THE STORYCRAFT WRITER'S JOURNAL

PLAN, PLOT, AND CREATE YOUR NEXT
NOVEL: HISTORICAL FICTION EDITION

VANESSA RILEY

GALLIUM BOOKS

© 2025 VANESSA RILEY

ALL RIGHTS RESERVED. NO PART OF THIS PUBLICATION MAY BE REPRODUCED, DISTRIBUTED, OR TRANSMITTED IN ANY FORM OR BY ANY MEANS, INCLUDING PHOTOCOPYING, RECORDING, OR OTHER ELECTRONIC OR MECHANICAL METHODS, WITHOUT THE PRIOR WRITTEN PERMISSION OF THE PUBLISHER, EXCEPT IN THE CASE OF BRIEF QUOTATIONS EMBODIED IN CRITICAL REVIEWS AND CERTAIN OTHER NONCOMMERCIAL USES PERMITTED BY COPYRIGHT LAW.

FIRST EDITION

ISBN 978-1-943885-37-4

COVER DESIGN BY V. G. RILEY

INTERIOR DESIGN BY V. G. RILEY

PRINTED IN THE UNITED STATES OF AMERICA

Foreword / Getting Started

Welcome!

This journal is designed to guide you step by step through the process of writing your next romance, women's fiction, or love story. We'll start by exploring some of the frameworks professional writers use, including Romancing the Beat, the 7 Stages of a RomCom (Romance Comedy), and Romantasy. These models help you structure your story, build meaningful characters, and create emotional arcs that resonate with readers.

Once we've reviewed these frameworks, I'll lead you through practical journaling exercises. These exercises are designed to help you craft your story piece by piece. As you work through them, we'll circle back to the methods so you can see how your writing connects to proven story structures.

The latter half of this journal is focused on weekly writing planning schedules—52 weeks of prompts and exercises to keep you moving forward. Whether you're a busy professional, a chronic procrastinator, or simply someone who wants a more organized approach to writing, this journal provides a concise method to help you finish your book.

We'll also use the Build-a-Character method, which guides you through understanding your protagonist from every angle: their values, desires, relationships, conflicts, and growth. Vanessa's YouTube series, Build-a-Character — 10 Sessions, complements this method and offers deeper explanations of each step.

This journal is for anyone who wants to write but struggles to find the time—or who wants a structured, inspiring, and achievable way to get their story on the page. Grab your pen, dive in, and let's get started!

About Vanessa Riley

Vanessa Riley is an acclaimed author known for captivating novels such as Island Queen, a Good Morning America Buzz Pick, and Queen of Exiles, an ABC View Lit Pick. She was honored as the 2024 Georgia Mystery/Detective Author of the year for Murder in Drury Lane and the 2023 Georgia Literary Fiction Author of the Year for Sister Mother Warrior. Her craft highlights hidden narratives of power, love, and sisterhoods of Black women and women of color in historical fiction, romance, and mystery genres. Her works have received praise from publications like the Washington Post, Entertainment Weekly, NPR, Publisher Weekly, and the New York Times.

In addition to penning over twenty-five novels, Vanessa holds a doctorate in mechanical engineering from Stanford University and STEM degrees from Penn State, adding a research-oriented approach to her writing process and inclusive storytelling.

Vanessa's Latest Books

Historical Fiction	Mystery Series	Romance
Fire Sword & Sea (2026) HarperCollins	Lady Worthing Mysteries: Murder in Westminster Kensington	A Gamble at Sunset Kensington
Queen of Exiles HarperCollins	Murder in Drury Lane Kensington	A Wager at Midnight Kensington
Sister Mother Warrior HarperCollins	Murder in Berkeley Square Kensington	A Deal at Dawn Kensington
Island Queen William Morrow	Murder in Whitehall (2027) Severn House	A Duke, The Lady, and A Baby Kensington
		An Earl, The Girl, and a Toddler Kensington
		A Duke, A Spy, an Artist, and a Lie Kensington

Connect on Socials and Subscribe to Write of Passage

- https://vanessariley.com
- https://www.instagram.com/vanessarileyauthor/
- https://www.youtube.com/@VanessaRileyAuthor
- https://vanessariley.substack.com/

ROMANCING THE BEATS

Romancing the Beat is a storytelling method specifically for writing romance novels. It breaks down the romantic story into a sequence of emotional beats—key moments that guide the development of the central love story. Each beat shows how the protagonists meet, resist, fall in love, face setbacks, and ultimately overcome obstacles to be together. At its core, it's about emotional progression: not just what happens externally in the plot, but how the characters' feelings evolve, how their false beliefs (lies) or fears are challenged, and how the romance grows authentically over the course of the story.

In essence, it answers the question: "How do two people go from strangers—or even antagonists—to fully committed lovers in a way that feels satisfying to the reader?"

TO-DO LIST

NOTES

Today's Mood

ROMANCING THE BEATS

TO-DO LIST

☐ ....
☐ ....
☐ ....
☐ ....
☐ ....
☐ ....
☐ ....

NOTES

Sources:
Bouricius, Ann. The Romance Readers' Advisory: The Librarian's Guide to Love in the Stacks. American Library Association.
Dyer, Lucinda. "Romance: In Its Own Time." Publishers Weekly, June 13, 2005.
Regis, Pamela. A Natural History of the Romance Novel. University of Pennsylvania Press.
Thurston, Carol. The Romance Revolution. University of Illinois Press.

Today's Mood

Historical Context:

The concept of structuring romantic narratives has deep historical roots. In the 17th century, Pierre Daniel Huet's Traité de l'origine des romans (1670) explored the origins and development of romance literature, emphasizing the role of love adventures in prose fiction. This treatise laid the groundwork for understanding the evolution of romantic storytelling.

In the 19th century, the genre of historical romance gained prominence, with authors like Lord Byron contributing to its popularity. This era saw the emergence of novels that blended romantic plots with historical settings, further shaping the trajectory of romantic fiction.

Gwen Hayes' Romancing the Beat can be seen as a contemporary evolution of these long-standing traditions, offering a modern, systematic approach to crafting romance narratives that resonate with today's readers.

ROMANCING THE BEATS

Phase 1: Set-Up (0–25% of story)

Chapter 1: Introduce H1
- Hook the reader with H1 in their everyday life.
- Show internal struggle or fear blocking love.
- Highlight H1's desires, flaws, and unique personality.
- Introduce external goal (promotion, vacation, artifact, etc.).
- Hint at what H1 needs (courage, patience, love, self-discovery).
- Placement: First 4-5% of story.

Chapter 2: Meet Cute
- H1 and H2 meet through external forces, chance, or crisis.
- Include instant attraction or immediate conflict/dislike.
- Make it memorable—something they'd recall years later.
- Hint at potential compatibility and obstacles.
- Placement: Around 5-8% of story.

Chapter 3: Introduce H2
- Show H2's slice of life, desires, flaws, and personality.
- Introduce H2's external goal and internal need.
- Throw in a "hitch" to make H2 compelling.
- Placement: 10-12% of story.

Chapter 4: No Way 1 (H1's Argument Against Love)
- H1 states (internally or externally) why love, especially with H2, is impossible.
- Tie the argument to H1's fears, false beliefs, or past experiences.
- Placement: 18-20% of story.

Chapter 5: Adhesion (Forced Together)
- Plot event forces H1 and H2 to work together.
- Cannot succeed without each other.
- Sparks and tension start; attraction begins to show despite resistance.
- Placement: Around 20% of story.

TO-DO LIST

NOTES

Today's Mood

ROMANCING THE BEATS

TO-DO LIST

NOTES

Today's Mood

Chapter 6: No Way 2
- H1 doubles down on resisting love.
- Conflict between H1's external goal and internal needs becomes clearer.
- Placement: 25% mark.

Chapter 7: Inkling of Desire
- Attraction grows; H1's false beliefs are challenged.
- Include small moments that reveal H1/H2's deeper sides.
- Placement: 30% mark.

Chapter 8: Deepening Desire
- Characters show glimpses of true selves.
- Internal and external actions further erode false beliefs.
- Placement: 40% mark.

Chapter 9: Maybe This Could Work
- H1 and H2 reconsider earlier resistance.
- Begin questioning "No Way" arguments.
- Internal and external conflicts create tension.
- Placement: 45% mark.
- Chapter 10: Midpoint of Love
- False high: everything seems possible—love and goals can coexist.
- Goals appear within reach; reader senses temporary resolution.
- Placement: 50% mark.

ROMANCING THE BEATS

Phase 2: Falling in Love (25–50% of story)

Chapter 11: Inkling of Doubt
- Past fears resurface; H1/H2 pull back slightly.
- Tie doubt to their No Way beliefs.
- Placement: 55% mark.

Chapter 12: Deepening Doubt
- Intimacy grows but doubts start to poke through.
- Expand tension from previous beat.
- Placement: 60% mark.

Chapter 13: Retreat Beat
- Characters express fears and begin emotionally withdrawing.
- Trust falters; internal conflicts clash with growing desire.
- Placement: 65–70% mark.

Chapter 14: Shields Up
- H1's worst fears materialize; relationship seems doomed.
- Shows the true weight of their No Way arguments.
- Placement: 70–75% mark.

Chapter 15: Break Up
- Characters revert fully to old beliefs/fears.
- Relationship ends, darkest emotional moment.
- Stakes are high for reconciliation later.
- Placement: 75% mark.

TO-DO LIST

NOTES

Today's Mood

ROMANCING THE BEATS

Phase 4: Fighting for Love (75–100% of story)

TO-DO LIST

NOTES

Today's Mood

Chapter 16: Dark Night
- H1/H2 reflect on mistakes, past joys, and what's at stake.
- Reader sees potential path to reconciliation.
- Placement: 80% mark.

Chapter 17: Wake Up
- Protagonist chooses love over fear.
- Tension rises as they act to fix the relationship.
- Placement: 85% mark.

Chapter 18: Grand Gesture
- Big, bold act proves commitment and love.
- Resolve external challenges alongside relationship.
- Placement: 85-90% mark.

Chapter 19: What Wholehearted Looks Like
- Show transformed protagonists fully embracing love.
- Resolve arcs, internal and external conflicts.
- Reward readers for emotional journey.
- Placement: 95% mark.

Chapter 20: Epilogue
- Characters return to "ordinary world" with new perspectives.
- Optional: hint at future conflicts or series continuation.
- Placement: 98-100% mark.

7 ROM-COM BEATS

The 7 Rom-Com Beats or Seven Romantic Comedy Beats is a screenwriting structure introduced by Billy Mernit in his 2000 book, Writing the Romantic Comedy. Drawing from his experience as a romance novelist and a story analyst for Hollywood studios, Mernit identified seven pivotal moments that define the emotional and narrative arc of romantic comedies. These beats serve as a guide for writers to craft engaging and emotionally resonant rom-coms.

Origins and Development
Billy Mernit, a former Harlequin romance novelist, transitioned into a career as a story analyst for major Hollywood studios. In his book, Writing the Romantic Comedy, Mernit analyzed successful romantic comedies and distilled their structures into seven essential beats:

1. The Chemical Equation (Setup) - Introduces the protagonist's internal and/or external conflict, establishing the status quo and hinting at underlying issues.
2. Meet Cute (The Catalyst) - The inciting incident that brings the protagonist and love interest together, often under humorous or unusual circumstances.
3. A Sexy Complication (Turning Point 1) - A development that raises the stakes and clearly defines the protagonist's external goal, often setting the protagonist and love interest at cross-purposes.

TO-DO LIST

NOTES

Today's Mood

7 ROM-COM BEATS

TO-DO LIST

NOTES

Today's Mood

- The Hook (Midpoint) – A situation that irrevocably binds the protagonist with the love interest, altering perspectives and increasing romantic tension.
- Swivel (Turning Point 2) – The stakes reach their highest point, and the romantic relationship's importance jeopardizes the protagonist's chance to succeed at their stated goal.
- Dark Moment (Crisis Climax) – The "all is lost" moment where everything seems to fall apart, and the relationship and/or the protagonist's goal is seemingly lost forever.
- Joyful Defeat (Resolution) – The protagonist and love interest reconcile, reaffirming the importance of the relationship, often at the cost of some personal sacrifice.

Mernit's framework adapts the traditional three-act structure specifically for romantic comedies, emphasizing the unique emotional journey that defines the genre. This structure has been widely adopted by writers and analysts to craft compelling romantic narratives.

Sources:
Writing the Romantic Comedy by Billy Mernit
7 Romantic Comedy Beats: Rom-Com Plot Structure Gold on Plottr
Anatomy of a Romantic Comedy — Seven Essential Story Beats on Well-Storied

7 ROM-COM BEATS

Phase 1: Setup and The Catalyst

Chapter 1: The Chemical Equation (Setup)

Introduce the Protagonist and their ordinary world. Show how they navigate daily life, but hint at something "off" or unsatisfying. Establish their internal conflict (fears, false beliefs, or insecurities) and external goals (career, travel, personal ambition). Introduce the stakes and what might be holding them back from love.

Purpose:
- Show the Protagonist's current life and dissatisfaction.
- Introduce goals and desires that will conflict with the Love Interest.
- Make the character relatable and three-dimensional.

Breakdown:
- Act 1 = 25% of the story.
- Setup/Hook = ~12-13% of story, midway through Act 1.

Chapter 2: Meet Cute (The Catalyst)
Phase 1: Catalyst / Inciting Incident (End of Act 1)
The Protagonist and Love Interest meet through an amusing, unexpected, or high-stakes situation. There may be instant attraction—or more often, instant dislike. Introduce the root of their conflict, social clash, or misunderstanding.

Purpose:
- Create tension and humor.
- Set the stage for their intertwined journeys.
- Hint at potential chemistry and obstacles.

Breakdown:
- Act 1 = 25% of story.
- Meet Cute / Inciting Incident = ~25% mark.

TO-DO LIST

NOTES

Today's Mood

7 ROM-COM BEATS

Phase 2: Rising Action and Pre-Crisis

Chapter 3: A Sexy Complication (Turning Point 1)
Phase 2: Rising Action (Act 2 Beginning)
Introduce a complication that raises the stakes and puts the Protagonist's external goal at odds with their internal needs or the Love Interest. Characters begin to see each other differently, creating romantic tension and conflict.
Purpose:
- Highlight conflicting desires and growing attraction.
- Raise the stakes through external and internal obstacles.
- Begin character development through interactions.

Breakdown:
- Act 2 = 50% of story (25%-75%).
- Turning Point 1 = ~25% mark, beginning of Act 2.

Chapter 4: The Hook (Midpoint)
Phase 2: Midpoint / Raising the Stakes (Middle of Act 2)
The Protagonist and Love Interest are forced together in a situation that heightens emotions, tension, or sexual attraction. This event challenges the Protagonist's beliefs and forces a "what if" consideration of the relationship.
Purpose:
- Strengthen emotional connection and stakes.
- Test characters' internal conflicts and external goals.
- Give readers a "this could work... but no" moment.

Breakdown:
- Midpoint occurs around 50% mark of Act 2.

Chapter 5: Swivel (Turning Point 2)
Phase 2 / 3: Pre-Crisis (End of Act 2)
The Protagonist and Love Interest share intimacy—emotional, physical, or relational. Stakes peak as the romance now threatens their goals. The relationship deepens, but conflict remains between love and ambition or other priorities.
Purpose:
- Show deepening relationship and its consequences.
- Heighten tension and suspense for readers.

Breakdown:
- Act 2 = 25%-75% of story.
- Turning Point 2 (Swivel) = ~60-62% mark.

7 ROM-COM BEATS

Phase 3: All is Lost and Phase 4: Reconciliation

Chapter 6: Dark Moment (Crisis / Climax)
Phase 3: All Is Lost (Beginning of Act 3)
The "darkest moment" occurs. Misunderstandings, betrayals, or external pressures make reconciliation seem impossible. Internal fears and false beliefs resurface. Both Protagonist and Love Interest face consequences that threaten goals and love.
Purpose:
- Create maximum tension and emotional stakes.
- Force reflection and character growth.
- Prepare the stage for reconciliation.

Breakdown:
- Act 3 = final 25% of story.
- Dark Moment / Crisis = ~75% mark.

Chapter 7: Joyful Defeat (Resolution)
Phase 4: Reconciliation / Happy Ending (End of Act 3)
The Protagonist and Love Interest choose love over fear, misbeliefs, or external goals. They apologize, reconcile, and sacrifice for love. Internal and external conflicts are resolved, showing how the characters have transformed.
Purpose:
- Deliver satisfying emotional closure.
- Highlight character growth and relational triumph.
- Reinforce the theme of love's transformative power.

Breakdown:
- Resolution / Joyful Defeat = ~88%-98% mark.
- End of Act 3 = ~100% of story.

TO-DO LIST

NOTES

Today's Mood

ROMANTASY BEATS

Romantasy refers to stories where romance is central, and the fantasy elements (magic, worldbuilding, supernatural stakes, political intrigue, etc.) are not just backdrop but tightly interwoven with the emotional stakes of the romance. The plot would fall apart without the romance—remove the romantic arc, and the story loses its emotional core.

Romantasy Beats
World & Protagonist Setup
Meet of Love & Catalyst
First Resistance / "No Way"
Forced Cooperation / World Stakes Raise
Deepening Connection + Fantasy Conflict
Midpoint / False Hope
Betrayal or Dark Revelation
Separation / Retreat
Dark Night / Lowest Point
Wake-Up & Grand Gesture
Resolution / Heroic Sacrifice & Love Triumphs
Aftermath & Epilogue

ROMANTASY BEATS

Phase 2: Setup / Hook (Act 2)

Beat	What Happens (Romance + Fantasy Layer)	
World & Protagonist Setup	Introduce H1 in their fantasy world: magic, rules, conflicts. Show their external goal and internal wounds. Establish what the fantasy risk is (war, magical imbalance, prophecy, etc.).	
Meet of Love & Catalyst	H1 meets H2 (or is forced into proximity) through some fantasy event (e.g., curse, magical accident, alliance necessity). The catalyst disturbs both personal and world status quo.	
First Resistance / "No Way"	H1 resists romance due to internal beliefs/fears, responsibilities, or because romance conflicts with fantasy duty (e.g., prophecy states love must be sacrificed).	
Forced Cooperation / World Stakes Raise	External fantasy plot pushes them together—maybe to solve a magical problem, fight a common enemy, or undertake a quest. Their romantic chemistry starts under duress.	

Today's Mood

ROMANTASY BEATS

Beat	What Happens (Romance + Fantasy Layer)	
Deepening Connection + Fantasy Conflict	They share vulnerability; fantasy stakes magnify (e.g. one's magic is dangerous or unstable). Conflict between what they want romantically vs what the world demands.	
Midpoint / False Hope	A turning point where both romance & fantasy goals seem aligned—maybe a victory or breakthrough that suggests they might have both love and save the world.	
Betrayal or Dark Revelation	Something is revealed about fantasy world rules, past betrayals, or magical curses that threatens trust or loyalty. The romantic relationship is tested heavily.	
Separation / Retreat	The lovers are pulled apart—geographically, magically, by duty, or by misunderstanding. Each faces what losing the other would cost them, and goes back into guarding or shielding hearts.	

ROMANTASY BEATS

Beat	What Happens (Romance + Fantasy Layer)	
Dark Night / Lowest Point	All seems lost—fantasy stakes are dire, the personal cost is huge. H1 (or both) must reckon with internal fears, false beliefs, sacrifice.	
Wake-Up & Grand Gesture	One or both make a conscious choice to fight for love despite the fantasy cost. Might involve magic, risking life, rejecting prophecy, breaking rules, etc.	
Resolution / Heroic Sacrifice & Love Triumphs	Fantasy threats resolved (as much as the story allows); romantic relationship solidified, internal arcs healed; authors show how both leads changed.	
Aftermath & Epilogue	Return to (new) ordinary world or status quo. Show the consequences in the fantasy world of their choices. Demonstrate the lasting change in both protagonists and in their world.	

Today's Mood

TROPES

Writing Considerations

A trope is a recurring theme, motif, plot device, character type, or narrative convention that is recognizable within a genre. Tropes are the building blocks of storytelling—they act as familiar patterns or shortcuts that convey meaning quickly to the reader.

- Examples: "The Reluctant Hero" in fantasy, "Locked Room Murder" in mystery, or "The Mentor" in adventure stories.

Why Tropes Matter
1. Reader Expectations – Tropes signal genre and style, helping readers understand what type of story they're engaging with.
2. Structure & Pacing – Tropes provide a scaffolding for plot progression and character development.
3. Emotional Resonance – Tropes evoke familiar emotions and responses, making a story relatable.
4. Creative Opportunities – Tropes can be used, subverted, or twisted to surprise readers or provide depth.
5. Marketability – Recognizable tropes can make a book more appealing to target audiences.

Today's Mood

TROPES

Tropes as a Catalyst

When Writers Should Consider Tropes
- Before Plotting (Planning Stage)
  - Identify which tropes are common in your genre.
  - Decide which tropes you want to use, avoid, or subvert.
  - Helps shape genre conventions, tone, and story structure.
- During Plotting (Outlining Stage)
  - Use tropes as story beats or narrative anchors.
  - Ensure character arcs align with or intentionally challenge familiar tropes.
  - Helps maintain pacing and reader engagement.
- During Writing (Drafting Stage)
  - Tropes can guide scene creation or dialogue.
  - They help in crafting reader expectations and building tension.
  - Writers can choose when to lean on, twist, or avoid tropes for surprise or originality.
- During Editing / Revising Stage
  - Assess whether tropes are overused, underdeveloped, or could be subverted.
  - Ensure the story feels fresh while still satisfying genre conventions.

TO-DO LIST

NOTES

Today's Mood

TROPES

Writing Considerations

Which tropes do you like and why?

Today's Mood

TROPES

Romance Tropes

Now let's look at the many romance tropes.

- Accidental Adultery – A character unknowingly has an affair (e.g., they didn't know the love interest was married, or the marriage wasn't valid).
- Accidental Pregnancy – An unexpected pregnancy becomes the central complication or bonding point in the romance.
- Age Gap – Older Hero / Younger Heroine – The man is significantly older than the woman, creating tension around experience, maturity, and power dynamics.
- Age Gap – Younger Hero / Older Heroine – The woman is older, often playing with themes of confidence, societal judgment, or role reversal.
- Alpha Male – A dominant, powerful, protective, and often bossy male lead.
- Already Married – The couple is already married, but love (or conflict) develops or redevelops during the story.
- Amnesia – One character loses their memory, creating romantic tension when rediscovering their identity or relationship.
- Antihero – The love interest is morally gray, flawed, or unconventional but still compelling.
- Arranged Marriage – Families or social situations force the couple to marry, love comes after.
- Asshole Hero – The hero is rude, cocky, or abrasive but eventually softens or redeems himself.
- Baby on Doorstep – A baby unexpectedly enters the couple's life, forcing them into caregiving and closeness.

THESE INTEREST ME

- _____
- _____
- _____
- _____
- _____
- _____
- _____

NOTES

_____
_____
_____
_____
_____
_____
_____
_____
_____
_____

Today's Mood

TROPES

Romance Tropes

- Back from the Dead – A love interest thought dead returns, creating shock, reunion, or conflict.
- Baker Romance – One or both love interests work in baking, coffee shops, or cozy food settings.
- Band of Brothers – A group of male friends or comrades-in-arms form the backdrop of the romance.
- BDSM – The romance features bondage, discipline, dominance, submission, sadism, and/or masochism.
- Beauty and the Beast – One partner is outwardly intimidating, scarred, or beastly but tender inside.
- Best Friend Triangle – Two friends love the same person, or a best friend complicates the romance.
- Best Friend's Older Brother – The heroine falls for her best friend's protective, tempting brother.
- Beta in the Streets/Alpha in the Sheets – The hero appears kind, supportive, or easygoing in public but is dominant and passionate privately.
- Betty & Veronica Triangle – A love triangle with two very different rivals for affection (sweet vs. sultry, good girl vs. bad girl).
- Big Gesture Apology – A dramatic act of love or sacrifice to win forgiveness.
- Billionaire – The love interest is fabulously wealthy, with romance involving luxury and power.
- Billionaire Playboy – Wealthy and notorious for casual affairs until he meets "the one."
- Bisexual Hero/ine – A bisexual character's sexuality is acknowledged as part of their romantic journey.
- Blackmail – One character coerces another (into marriage, dating, etc.) with leverage.
- Blackmail Date – Similar, but the coercion is specifically around going on dates or spending time together.
- Blind Date – The couple meets on a setup arranged by friends or services.
- Blind Date Mixup – A mistaken identity twist where the wrong people end up paired.
- Blue Collar – The love interest is a working-class character (mechanic, builder, plumber, etc.), often contrasted with someone wealthier.
- Bodyguard – A protector is hired and romance sparks with the one being protected.

TROPES

Romance Tropes

- Boss/Employee – Workplace romance where one character has authority over the other.
- Boss/Nanny – A single parent falls for the nanny hired to care for their child.
- Boyfriend/Girlfriend's Best Friend – Romance develops between someone and their partner's best friend.
- Break Their Heart to Save Them – One character pushes the other away "for their own good," even though they're still in love.
- Breakup Due to Misunderstanding – The couple breaks up over miscommunication or mistaken assumptions.
- Brother's Best Friend – A heroine falls for her brother's protective or tempting best friend.
- Bully Romance – A former (or current) bully becomes the love interest, often set in high school/college.
- Captive Falls for Captor – Stockholm Syndrome-style romance where the kidnapped falls for the kidnapper.
- Caretaker / Nursed Back to Health – One character tends to the other during illness or injury, deepening intimacy.
- Celebrity/Ordinary Person – A famous figure falls for someone from outside the spotlight.
- Celibate Hero – The hero is abstinent (for religious, personal, or trauma reasons) until the heroine.
- Child Free – The couple chooses not to have children, and the romance supports that.
- Child Instigates Breakup – A child (their own or someone else's) creates the conflict that separates the couple.
- Childhood Friends – Long-term friends grow into something more.

THESE INTEREST ME

NOTES

Today's Mood

TROPES

Romance Tropes

- Childhood Friends Reunion – Childhood friends meet again later in life and rekindle closeness.
- Childhood Marriage Pact – A promise made in youth ("If we're both single at 30, we'll marry") sets up the romance.
- Childhood Sweethearts – A first love that endures or rekindles after time apart.
- Childhood Trauma – Past childhood pain affects one or both characters, shaping their love story.
- Chosen One – A destined or prophesied lover/partner, often in fantasy or paranormal romance.
- Cinderella (Story/Wrong Side of the Tracks) – Poor or overlooked heroine finds love with someone wealthy or powerful.
- Cinderella Circumstance (Duke and Governess or Maid) – Historical-specific version where class difference (servant + nobility) drives the romance.
- Class Differences (Ton vs. Servants) – In historical romance, a noble falls for someone serving them.
- Class Differences (Ton vs. Working Class) – A noble or wealthy figure loves someone from the lower working classes.
- Coach's Daughter – Falling for the coach's child, often taboo in sports settings.
- Coming Out – A romance entwined with a character's journey of acknowledging or revealing their sexuality.
- Commoner/Aristocrat – A modern or historical class-clash romance between everyday person and nobility.
- Compromised Heroine – In historical romance, a woman's reputation is endangered, often forcing marriage with the hero.
- Cooking Show Romance – Love develops during a televised competition or cooking program.
- Courtly Love – A medieval-style romance of knights and noble ladies, often involving unrequited or idealized passion.
- Cowboy/Ranchers – Romance centered in Western/rural ranch life.
- Dark Romance – Assassin – A morally dark romance featuring a killer as the love interest.
- Dark Romance – Blackmailer – Love interest coerces or manipulates through threats but romance develops.
- Dark Romance – Kidnapper – Kidnapping drives the setup for an intense, taboo romance.

TROPES

Romance Tropes

- Dark Romance – Kidnapper – Kidnapping drives the setup for an intense, taboo romance.
- Destitute Hero/ine – A lead is impoverished, which impacts the romance (rescue fantasy, rags-to-riches).
- Dogs Are Great – Pets, especially dogs, play a big role in bringing the couple together.
- Dystopian – Romance takes place in a broken or oppressive future society.
- Enemies to Lovers – Two characters who clash and hate each other grow into love.
- Epistolary – Romance told through letters, emails, texts, or diary entries.
- Ex of MC is Hanging Around – An ex causes tension or drama by lingering in the picture.
- Extended Breakup – The couple separates for a long period before reconciling.
- Fairytale – The romance mirrors a classic fairytale structure or aesthetic.
- Fake Courtship (Historical Romance) – Pretend dating/marriage in a historical setting, often to protect reputations.
- Fake Death – One character fakes their death, leading to angst and reunion.
- Fake Engagement – A couple pretends to be engaged for convenience or external reasons, but real feelings spark.
- Fake Relationship – A pretend romance arrangement that evolves into the real thing.
- Fallen Woman – A heroine whose reputation is ruined (unwed pregnancy, scandal, etc.) finds love despite stigma.

THESE INTEREST ME

NOTES

Today's Mood

TROPES

Romance Tropes

- False Pretenses – One character deceives the other about identity, job, or intentions.
- Family Saga – The romance is part of a multigenerational family-centered story.
- Famous but Unrecognized – A celebrity goes incognito, and the love interest doesn't know who they are.
- Farm/Ranch Life – Set in agricultural/rural settings, grounded in nature and hard work.
- Fated Mates – Common in paranormal romance—two souls destined for each other.
- Female Friendship Group – A central group of women support each other's love journeys.
- First Love – Focus on experiencing or rekindling that very first romance.
- Forced Proximity – Characters stuck together in close quarters (elevator, snowstorm, stranded, etc.).
- Friends to Enemies to Lovers – A shifting dynamic: friends → fallout → rediscovered passion.
- Friends to Lovers – Longtime pals slowly realize their bond is romantic.
- Friends with Benefits – Two friends add sex to their relationship, expecting no feelings—but love grows.
- Friends with Benefits / No Strings Attached – A casual fling arrangement that evolves into love.
- Friendship Group – A circle of friends, where multiple romances may form across books in a series.
- Gaming Club – Love blossoms around tabletop/online/video gaming communities.
- Grumpy/Sunshine Dynamic – One character is sour, stoic, or broody while the other is cheerful and warm.
- Guardian/Ward – Historical trope where a guardian becomes romantically involved with their charge.
- Harem of Friends – A central character is surrounded by multiple friends/love interests competing or sharing.
- Hate to Love You – Close cousin of enemies to lovers, but more playful banter and chemistry-driven.
- Hero All In from the Beginning – The hero is steadfastly committed right away, even if the heroine resists.

TROPES

Romance Tropes

- Hero/ine in Relationship at Start – Story begins with one or both characters already dating someone else.
- Hero/ine with Self-Esteem Issues – A character struggles with low confidence or body image as part of the romance.
- Hero/ine with F'd up Parents – Dysfunctional families shape the character's baggage and growth in love.
- Heroine Disguised as Man – Heroine hides her gender for safety, work, or adventure, sparking hidden romance.
- Heroine Gives Herself as Payment – Heroine sacrifices herself to pay off a debt or bargain.
- Heroine in a "Male" Profession – A woman in a male-dominated field (soldier, scientist, firefighter) finds love.
- Heroine Owes Hero – Debt or obligation ties the heroine to the hero, creating imbalance and tension.
- Heroine Pursues Hero – Role reversal: the heroine actively chases the reluctant hero.
- Heroine with Sexual Confidence – Heroine is experienced, bold, or self-assured in intimacy.
- Hidden or Mistaken Identity – One character hides who they are, creating tension when truth comes out.
- High School Sweethearts – A romance that started in high school and either endures or rekindles later.
- Holiday Romance – Love story set around Christmas, Valentine's, or other holidays.
- Infertility – Struggles with conceiving or carrying children play into the emotional stakes.
- Interfering Family – Relatives meddle in the romance, creating drama or comedy.
- Jilted Bride/Groom – A wedding is called off, and love arises from the fallout.

THESE INTEREST ME

NOTES

Today's Mood

TROPES

Romance Tropes

- Jock Falls for Nerdy Tutor – Athletic, popular guy falls for academically focused, "nerdy" tutor or classmate.
- Kidnapping – One character is abducted, often leading to danger-driven or intense romance.
- Lady's Companion – Historical trope: the heroine is a governess, lady's maid, or companion, often falling for her employer.
- Ladykiller in Love – A notorious flirt or rake unexpectedly falls for one person genuinely.
- Long Distance Relationship – Romance persists despite geographic separation.
- Love at First Sight – Immediate, intense attraction that drives the romance.
- Love Coach – One character mentors another in love or dating.
- Love Letters – Romance communicated or built through letters or notes.
- Love Letters – Secret Admirer – One character writes secretly to the other, building mystery and affection.
- Love Triangle – Three characters entangled romantically, with competition or tension.
- Loving Thy Neighbor – Romance between people living near each other, often with humor or tension.
- Mafia / Organized Crime – Romance set within criminal organizations; can include danger, power, and taboo.
- Mail Order Bride – Historical or modern: a woman travels to marry someone she has never met.
- Marriage of Convenience – Characters marry for practical reasons (money, inheritance, reputation) but fall in love.
- Mars Needs Women – Sci-fi romance trope where alien/martian context brings a hero and heroine together.
- Matchmaker – Romance arises through the schemes of a friend, relative, or professional matchmaker.
- Matchmaker Crush – One character sets others up, only to realize they have feelings themselves.
- Mating/Bonding – Paranormal trope, often shifters, with destined pairings or psychic bonds.
- Menage – A romance with three people (MFM, MMF, etc.) in a consensual relationship.
- Mental Health Issues – Characters face depression, anxiety, PTSD, or other conditions impacting the romance.

TROPES

Romance Tropes

- Mentorship – One character guides the other professionally or personally, building closeness.
- Military Life – Romance set in the military context, with deployments, duty, and camaraderie.
- Military Romance – Often emphasizes danger, heroism, and long-distance challenges.
- Mistaken Identity – Characters are confused for someone else, creating tension or comedic situations.
- Mistaken/False Identity – One character deliberately assumes a false persona.
- Motorcycle Club – Romance within biker culture; can include danger, loyalty, and alpha dynamics.
- Movie Star Falls for Commoner – Celebrity falls for someone "ordinary," often hidden from paparazzi.
- Multiples – MFF – A romance involving one man and two women.
- Multiples – MFM – One woman and two men in a consensual relationship.
- Multiples – MM – Two men together (usually with a single love interest).
- Multiples – MMF – Two men and one woman in a consensual romance.
- Navy SEALs – Romance featuring military elite, often focused on heroism, danger, and protectiveness.
- Nerd/Jock – A "brainy" character paired with an athletic one, often opposites attract.
- New Old Flame – An ex or past love reappears, rekindling old feelings.
- Obsessive Hero – A hero with an intense, sometimes possessive fixation on the heroine.
- Office Romance – Competition / Rivals – Two colleagues competing professionally while romance develops.

THESE INTEREST ME

NOTES

Today's Mood

TROPES

Romance Tropes

- Office Romance – Coworkers with Benefits – Workplace fling that evolves into emotional connection.
- Older Couple – Romance between characters significantly older, often second-chance or mature love.
- Older Man / Younger Woman – Age gap trope emphasizing experience and mentorship/romance tension.
- Older Woman / Younger Man – Role reversal of the above, often exploring societal expectations.
- On a Journey – Romance develops while traveling, adventuring, or moving locations.
- On the Run – Characters escape danger, with romance intensifying during flight.
- One Night of Danger – Short, thrilling encounter sparks a longer romance.
- One Night Stand – Casual sex between characters that leads to emotional complications or love.
- Opposites – Bad Boy / Good Girl – Classic trope of danger and morality clashing with attraction.
- Opposites – Grumpy / Sunshine – One broody, one cheerful character, balancing each other.
- Opposites – Playboy / Virgin – Experienced and carefree partner paired with innocent or inexperienced one.
- Opposites Attract – Broad trope where personalities, lifestyles, or values clash but love develops.
- Orphan – A character without parents, often shaping independence or vulnerability in romance.
- Orphan Bonding – Orphans or abandoned characters find connection and love with each other.
- Outcast from Society – A marginalized or ostracized character finds romance despite prejudice.
- Overprotective Brother / Male Relatives – Male family members interfere to protect the heroine.
- Overprotective Sister / Female Relatives – Female relatives create obstacles or comedy in the romance.
- Past Coming Back to Haunt Them – A character's previous relationships, mistakes, or secrets create tension in the romance.
- Penpal Enemy – Characters correspond (letters/emails) while disliking each other in real life.

TROPES

Romance Tropes

- Pining After Child's Teacher – Parent develops romantic feelings for their child's educator.
- Pirate / Underworld King – Hero is a literal pirate or powerful figure in criminal/underworld settings.
- Plain Jane – An "average" or overlooked heroine who wins the hero's love.
- Playboy / Rake – Charming, promiscuous male lead who eventually commits to one love.
- Polyamory Love – Romance involving more than two consenting adults in a relationship.
- Possessive Hero – Hero displays strong protectiveness and sometimes jealousy over the heroine.
- Prank Date – A playful trick or setup leads to a romantic encounter.
- Puppy Hero – A sweet, loyal, gentle hero who contrasts with typical alpha traits.
- Rags to Royalty – A poor or commoner character rises socially or romantically, often marrying into nobility.
- Redemption – A flawed or morally gray character seeks redemption through love.
- Relationship Coach – One character teaches the other how to navigate love or dating.
- Rescue Romance – One character saves the other from danger, creating intimacy.
- Return to Hometown – Hero or heroine revisits their past, rekindling old romance.
- Revenge Journey – A character seeks revenge, and love complicates or redeems the path.
- Revenge Romance – Romance begins as part of a plan for revenge but evolves into real love.
- Reverse Harem – One female lead romantically involved with multiple men.
- Rich / Poor Dynamic (Money Dynamic Huge) – Wealth disparity is central to tension and attraction.

THESE INTEREST ME

NOTES

Today's Mood

TROPES

Romance Tropes

- Road Trip – Journeying together sparks romance, adventure, or discovery.
- Road Trip Romance – Same as above but with focus on romantic and emotional bonding.
- Rockstar Romance – Musician's fame, tours, and lifestyle create backdrop for romance.
- Romance on Set – Romance develops while filming, performing, or during production work.
- Romeo/Juliet – Lovers face external forces (family, society) trying to keep them apart.
- Roommate Romance – Living together arrangement leads to unexpected love.
- Royalty – A prince, princess, duke, or monarch is part of the romance.
- Royalty Falls for Commoner – Classic fairy-tale trope where royalty and ordinary person fall in love.
- Runaway Fiancé – One partner flees the wedding, causing romance, tension, or comedic situations.
- Scarred Hero/ine – Physical or emotional scars create tension, vulnerability, or attraction.
- Scavenger Hunt Bonding – Characters participate in a challenge or hunt that brings them closer.
- Second Chance Romance – Former lovers reunite to rekindle their relationship.
- Secret Admirer – One character expresses love anonymously, creating mystery and tension.
- Secret Baby – A child is kept hidden, causing complications when revealed.
- Secret Heir – A character discovers they are heir to a fortune, kingdom, or title.
- Secret Identity – Characters hide their true selves, often leading to misunderstanding or reveal.
- Secret Lovechild – A hidden child exists, often affecting inheritance, relationships, or scandal.
- Secret Relationship – The couple hides their romance from friends, family, or the public.
- Secret Waiting to Tear Them Apart – A hidden truth threatens to destroy the relationship.
- Sex Club – Setting or plot involves organized sexual encounters with multiple participants.
- Sex First / Feelings Later – Physical intimacy occurs before emotional attachment develops.

TROPES

Romance Tropes

- Sex Worker / Escort – One character works in sex services, creating tension or stigma in romance.
- Sibling Triangle – Two siblings compete for the same love interest or one falls for the other's partner.
- Single Parents / Guardian – One or both characters are raising children, adding stakes and bonding.
- Sleeping with the Boss – Workplace romance that begins or includes sexual encounters with a superior.
- Sleeping with the Teacher – Romance between student and teacher (taboo, often with power dynamics).
- Slow Seduction Due to Trauma – Romance builds gradually because one character has past trauma.
- Small Town – Close-knit community where everyone knows each other, affecting romance.
- Socially Awkward Hero – Hero struggles with social skills or confidence, often charmingly.
- Sociopathic Hero – Dark, morally ambiguous hero, often manipulative or dangerous.
- Sports – Romance set around athletic activities, events, or competitions.
- Sports Romance – Baseball – Specific romance involving baseball players or teams.
- Sports Romance – Basketball – Set in the basketball world.
- Sports Romance – Football / Rugby – Romance in football/rugby contexts.
- Sports Romance – Hockey – Set in the world of hockey.
- Sports Romance – Lacrosse – Focus on lacrosse players.
- Sports Romance – Soccer – Focus on soccer players.
- Sports Romance – Tennis Instructor – Romance with a tennis player or coach.

THESE INTEREST ME

- _____
- _____
- _____
- _____
- _____
- _____
- _____

NOTES

_____
_____
_____
_____
_____
_____
_____
_____
_____

Today's Mood

TROPES

Romance Tropes

- Sports Romance – Wrestling – Set in amateur or professional wrestling.
- Star-Crossed Love – Lovers thwarted by fate, circumstance, or family opposition.
- Step-sibling Crush – Romance develops between step-siblings (taboo or complicated).
- Story Told in Past and Present – Narrative alternates timelines, often revealing romance gradually.
- Stranded – Characters stuck together (island, storm, plane, etc.) sparks intimacy.
- Student / Teacher – Romance between student and teacher, often exploring power imbalance.
- Summer Romance – Short-term, often idyllic romance during a summer season.
- Surprise Pregnancy – Unexpected pregnancy affects the plot and emotional stakes.
- Surprise Virgin – Character's inexperience is revealed unexpectedly, often creating tension or humor.
- Survival – Characters survive extreme situations together, deepening their bond.
- Taboo Relationship / Forbidden Romance – Love prohibited by law, culture, family, or ethics.
- The Bet – Romance arises from a wager, challenge, or bet between characters.
- The Bodyguard – Love story between protector and the protected.
- The Doctor and Patient – Romance develops in medical context, often taboo or complicated.
- The Landscaper – Romance with a gardener/landscaper; often blue-collar vs. wealthy dynamic.
- The Lawyer and Client – Romantic tension emerges from legal representation.
- The Maid – Maid/nanny romance with employer or wealthy character.
- The Nanny – Similar to above; romance blossoms while caring for children.
- The No Feelings Hookup – Casual encounter intended to be without emotions, which evolves.
- The Pool Boy – Romance with a service worker, often in wealthy setting.
- The Rich and the Poor – Classic disparity-driven romance with socioeconomic tension.
- The Ugly Duckling / Ugly Duckling – Overlooked or "plain" character transformed by love.
- Time Travel – Romance across different eras or time periods.
- Too Dumb to Live – One character repeatedly makes foolish choices, often comedic or endearing.

TROPES

Romance Tropes

- Tortured Hero – Hero carries deep emotional or psychological pain affecting romance.
- Tragic Past – Characters' dark history shapes their romance.
- Tug-of-War Triangle – Love triangle with constant tension and back-and-forth between options.
- Two-person Love Triangle – Simplified triangle; two people caught in conflicted feelings.
- Ugly Hero / Heroine – Character is unconventional or unattractive by society's standards, yet finds love.
- Unrequited Love – One character loves another who doesn't (yet) return their feelings.
- Vampire-Werewolf Triangle – Paranormal romance involving a love triangle between supernatural beings.
- Vegas Wedding Surprise – Characters impulsively marry in Las Vegas, creating romantic and comedic tension.
- Villain Becomes Hero – Former antagonist redeems themselves through love.
- Virgin Auction – A character's virginity is wagered or sold, creating tension and romance.
- Virgin Hero – Inexperienced male lead navigates intimacy for the first time.
- Wartime Wedding – Romance develops against the backdrop of war, often urgent or emotional.
- Widow / Widower – Romance involving someone who has lost a spouse, often exploring grief and second chances.
- Workplace – Romance set in a professional environment, encompassing coworker, boss, or office dynamics.

THESE INTEREST ME

NOTES

Today's Mood

TROPES

Romance Tropes by Group

Enemies / Opposites / Tension
- Enemies to Lovers
- Hate to Love You
- Grumpy / Sunshine Dynamic
- Opposites Attract
- Opposites – Bad Boy / Good Girl
- Opposites – Grumpy / Sunshine
- Opposites – Playboy / Virgin
- Friends to Enemies to Lovers
- Tug-of-War Triangle

Friends / Childhood / Reunions
- Friends to Lovers
- Childhood Friends
- Childhood Friends Reunion
- Childhood Sweethearts
- First Love
- Best Friend Triangle
- Best Friend's Older Brother
- Boyfriend/Girlfriend's Best Friend
- Brother's Best Friend
- Friendship Group / Female Friendship Group
- New Old Flame

Workplace / Authority / Power
- Boss / Employee
- Sleeping with the Boss
- Office Romance – Coworkers with Benefits
- Office Romance – Competition / Rivals
- Boss / Nanny
- Heroine in a "Male" Profession
- The Lawyer and Client
- The Doctor and Patient
- Relationship Coach / Love Coach

TROPES

Romance Tropes by Group

Marriage / Family / Obligations
- Arranged Marriage
- Marriage of Convenience
- Fake Engagement
- Already Married
- Runaway Fiancé
- Jilted Bride/Groom
- Child Instigates Breakup
- Single Parents / Guardian
- Overprotective Brother / Male Relatives
- Overprotective Sister / Female Relatives

Taboo / Dark / Dangerous Romance
- Dark Romance - Assassin / Blackmailer / Kidnapper / Mafia
- Captive Falls for Captor
- Sociopathic Hero
- Taboo Relationship / Forbidden Romance
- Student / Teacher
- Step-sibling Crush
- Villain Becomes Hero
- Blackmail / Blackmail Date
- Obsessed / Possessive Hero
- Sex Worker / Escort

THESE INTEREST ME

NOTES

Today's Mood

TROPES

Romance Tropes by Group

Wealth / Class / Status
- Cinderella (Story / Circumstance)
- Royalty Falls for Commoner
- Commoner / Aristocrat
- Rich / Poor Dynamic
- Billionaire / Billionaire Playboy
- Destitute Hero/ine
- Famous but Unrecognized
- Mail Order Bride
- Rags to Royalty
- Class Differences (Ton vs Servants / Working Class)

Paranormal / Fantasy / Sci-Fi
- Fated Mates
- Chosen One
- Vampire-Werewolf Triangle
- Time Travel
- Mars Needs Women
- Mating / Bonding
- Reverse Harem / Menage / Polyamory Love
- Dark Romance - Mafia / Assassin (if supernatural variant)

Adventure / Travel / Danger
- Road Trip / Road Trip Romance
- Stranded / Survival
- On the Run
- On a Journey
- One Night of Danger
- Rescue Romance
- Pirate / Underworld King
- Scavenger Hunt Bonding

TROPES

Romance Tropes by Group

Comedy / Mistaken Identity / Playfulness
- Fake Relationship / Fake Courtship
- Fake Death
- Mistaken Identity / False Identity
- Prank Date
- Blind Date / Blind Date Mixup
- The Bet
- Too Dumb to Live

Secrets / Hidden Truths
- Secret Admirer
- Secret Baby / Secret Lovechild
- Secret Heir
- Secret Identity
- Secret Relationship
- Secret Waiting to Tear Them Apart
- Past Coming Back to Haunt Them

Romantic Gestures / Emotional Beats
- Big Gesture Apology
- Break Their Heart to Save Them
- Love at First Sight
- Slow Seduction Due to Trauma
- Hero All In from the Beginning
- Heroine Pursues Hero
- Love Letters / Secret Admirer Letters

Sports / Hobbies / Activities
- Sports (Baseball, Basketball, Football / Rugby, Hockey, Lacrosse, Soccer, Tennis Instructor, Wrestling)
- Gaming Club
- Coach's Daughter
- Cooking Show Romance
- Bakery / Baker Romance

THESE INTEREST ME

NOTES

Today's Mood

TROPES

Romance Tropes by Group

Holiday / Seasonal / Short-Term
- Summer Romance
- Holiday Romance
- Vegas Wedding Surprise
- Wartime Wedding

Trauma / Healing / Emotional Growth
- Hero / Heroine with F'd Up Parents
- Childhood Trauma
- Tragic Past
- Scarred Hero / Heroine
- Tortured Hero
- Infertility / Child Free
- Celibate Hero
- Mental Health Issues

Miscellaneous / Fun / Quirky
- Dogs Are Great
- Puppy Hero
- Ugly Duckling / Plain Jane / Ugly Hero / Heroine
- Cinderella Circumstance (Duke + Governess / Maid)
- Heroine Disguised as Man
- One Night Stand / Sex First / Feelings Later

Tropes

General Story Direction

Global Story

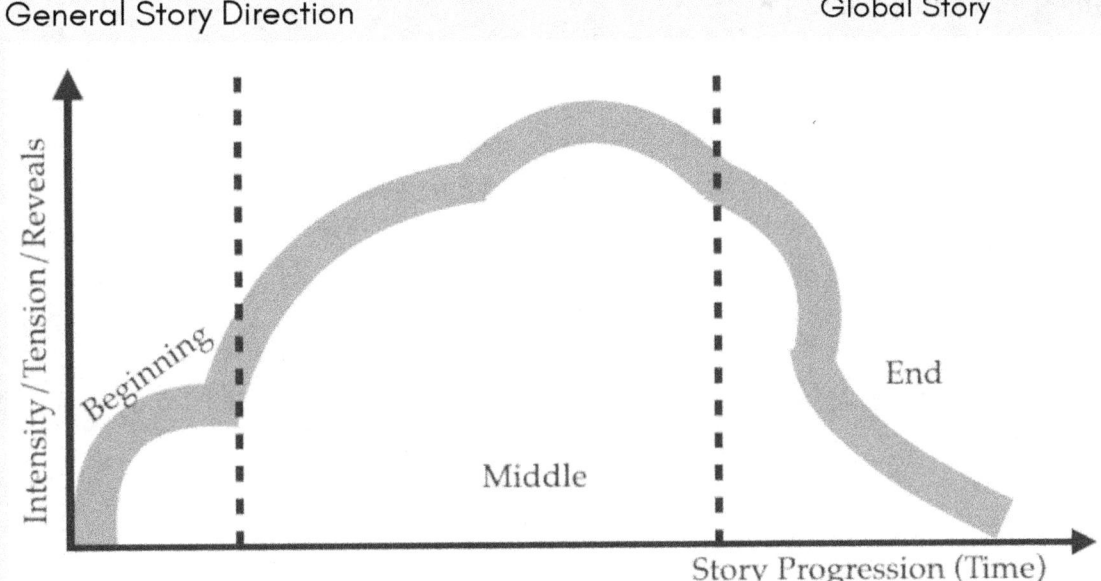

You can use more than one trope in a story, and tropes are powerful tools to drive the plot forward. Every genre has tropes—mysteries, thrillers, historical fiction, literary fiction, commercial fiction, and even nonfiction. Use them, play with them, and give them your own unique twists. Consider how a trope from one genre could add extra zing when applied to another. Romance tropes, in particular, are universal, familiar, and beloved by readers—they resonate because they tap into timeless patterns of desire, conflict, and connection. Embrace them, innovate with them, and let them enrich your storytelling.

Primary Trope:

Secondary Trope:

Additional Trope(s):

Write Draw Journal Craft Here

Story Arcs
Global Story

General Story Direction

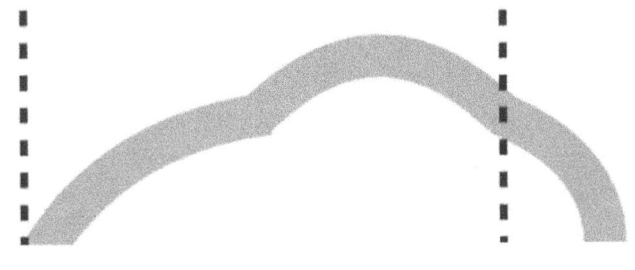

Prework Time

End:

Not Yet... Let's Do Some Prework
Every story needs a foundation. Use the next template pages to brainstorm. The work you do will carry your story forward."

Write Draw Journal Craft Here

THE SPARK

Prework for Your Story

In this section, introduce your protagonist and establish why their story matters — who they are, where they live, and a single day that reveals their rhythm.

TO-DO LIST

NOTES

Today's Mood

Write Draw Journal Craft Here

Names

List your favorite names for your story. Don't worry if they "fit" yet—just capture the ones that spark interest. Look up the meanings, origins, and associations (cultural, historical, symbolic). Note how these might connect to your character's personality, background, or fate. Experiment with variations (nicknames, shortened forms, translations). Sometimes the twist of a name unlocks a character. Consider sound and style—does it suit your genre? (e.g., "Lysandra" feels fantasy, while "Tommy" feels contemporary). Circle or highlight the names that feel strongest, then try them in a sentence or bit of dialogue to see if they come alive.

Name	Meaning	Nickname / Variants	Notes

Observations:

Write Draw Journal Craft Here

Attributes

Use this table to capture the key details of each of your characters. Fill in every row with what makes them visually distinct, their personality, quirks, goals, and everyday habits—anything that brings them to life on the page.

	Character Name	Character Name	Character Name
Attribute			
Eye Color			
Hair Color			
Gender			
Race/ Ethnicity			
Height			
Age			
Favorite Color			
Favorite Clothing			
Quirk			
Titles			
Profession			
Speech or Dialect			
Favorite Word(s)			
Country of Origin			

Write Draw Journal Craft Here

5 WHY'S

Journal Exercise: Digging Deeper into Motivations and Story Problems
Instructions:
1. Start with your character's surface goal (what they say they want).
2. Ask "Why?" and write the answer.
3. Ask "Why?" again—digging deeper each time.
4. Repeat at least 4-5 times until you reach an emotional or societal truth at the core.
5. This hidden truth is often where the real story tension lives.

Why is this story important?:

Why?:

Why?:

Why?:

Why?:

Observations:

Write Draw Journal Craft Here

5 WHY'S

Journal Exercise: Digging Deeper into Motivations and Story Problems

Instructions:
1. Start with your character's surface goal (what they say they want).
2. Ask "Why?" and write the answer.
3. Ask "Why?" again—digging deeper each time.
4. Repeat at least 4-5 times until you reach an emotional or societal truth at the core.
5. This hidden truth is often where the real story tension lives.

Why is this story important?:

Why?:

Why?:

Why?:

Why?:

Observations:

Write Draw Journal Craft Here

THE HEARTBEAT

Prework for Your Story

In this section, define characters' core values, beliefs, and desires — the invisible compass that drives their choices.

TO-DO LIST

NOTES

Today's Mood

Write Draw Journal Craft Here

Character Name: # Core Values

Journal Exercise: Core Values, Beliefs & Desires
Instructions:
Your character's core values and beliefs shape every decision they make—even when they don't realize it. Desires give them direction, while values and beliefs determine the choices they're willing (or unwilling) to make. Use the following questions to explore what guides your character deep down. Write freely, and don't be afraid to push for uncomfortable truths.

What principles would this character never compromise on, no matter the cost?

What does this character believe makes someone "good" or "honorable"?

What's more important to this character: truth, loyalty, or justice? Why?

Observations:

Write Draw Journal Craft Here

Character Name:

Beliefs

Journal Exercise: Core Values, Beliefs & Desires
Instructions:
Your character's core values and beliefs shape every decision they make—even when they don't realize it. Desires give them direction, while values and beliefs determine the choices they're willing (or unwilling) to make. Use the following questions to explore what guides your character deep down. Write freely, and don't be afraid to push for uncomfortable truths.

Does your character believe in God or has religious faith? Describe this system and how it affects actions or reactions.

Does this character believe people can truly change? Why or why not?

Does this character trust the world to be fair—or unfair? How does that belief show up in their actions?

Observations:

Write Draw Journal Craft Here

Character Name:

Desires

Journal Exercise: Core Values, Beliefs & Desires

Instructions:
Your character's core values and beliefs shape every decision they make—even when they don't realize it. Desires give them direction, while values and beliefs determine the choices they're willing (or unwilling) to make. Use the following questions to explore what guides your character deep down. Write freely, and don't be afraid to push for uncomfortable truths.

What does the character want most right now?

Does this character believe people can truly change? Why or why not?

What does this character think they need to be happy—and what do they really need?

Observations:

Write Draw Journal Craft Here

Character Name:

Core Values

Journal Exercise: Core Values, Beliefs & Desires
Instructions:
Your character's core values and beliefs shape every decision they make—even when they don't realize it. Desires give them direction, while values and beliefs determine the choices they're willing (or unwilling) to make. Use the following questions to explore what guides your character deep down. Write freely, and don't be afraid to push for uncomfortable truths.

What principles would this character never compromise on, no matter the cost?

What does this character believe makes someone "good" or "honorable"?

What's more important to this character: truth, loyalty, or justice? Why?

Observations:

Write Draw Journal Craft Here

Character Name: **Beliefs**

Journal Exercise: Core Values, Beliefs & Desires

Instructions:
Your character's core values and beliefs shape every decision they make—even when they don't realize it. Desires give them direction, while values and beliefs determine the choices they're willing (or unwilling) to make. Use the following questions to explore what guides your character deep down. Write freely, and don't be afraid to push for uncomfortable truths.

Does your character believe in God or has religious faith? Describe this system and how it affects actions or reactions.

Does this character believe people can truly change? Why or why not?

Does this character trust the world to be fair—or unfair? How does that belief show up in their actions?

Observations:

Write Draw Journal Craft Here

Character Name:

Desires

Journal Exercise: Core Values, Beliefs & Desires

Instructions:

Your character's core values and beliefs shape every decision they make—even when they don't realize it. Desires give them direction, while values and beliefs determine the choices they're willing (or unwilling) to make. Use the following questions to explore what guides your character deep down. Write freely, and don't be afraid to push for uncomfortable truths.

What does the character want most right now?

Does this character believe people can truly change? Why or why not?

What does this character think they need to be happy—and what do they really need?

Observations:

Write Draw Journal Craft Here

THE WEB

Prework for Your Story

In this section, map the relationships that matter (family, friends, mentors, rivals) and how those ties shape behavior and stakes.

TO-DO LIST

NOTES

Today's Mood

Write Draw Journal Craft Here

Character Name: # The Web

Journal Exercise: The Web — Mapping Your Character's Connections
Instructions:
Your character doesn't exist in isolation—the people around them shape who they are, how they act, and how their story unfolds. In this exercise, you'll create a relationship web to see your character's social universe at a glance.

Step 1: Draw the Web
- Write your character's name in the center of the page.
- Around the center, add names of people connected to your character:
  - Family members (parents, siblings, extended family)
  - Friends or allies
  - Mentors, guides, or teachers
  - Rivals, enemies, or antagonists

Step 2: Reflect on Influence
Ask yourself:
- How does each person influence your character?
- Who pushes them to grow or challenges their decisions?
- Who protects them, and who frustrates or opposes them?

Step 3: Label - Use arrows, notes, or symbols to show the type of relationship (supportive, tense, complicated, loving, competitive, etc.)
- S - Stranger (Beginning)
- L - Loath
- ♥ - Love
- FE - Frienemy
- F - Friend
- M - Mom
- D - Dad
- S - Sibling
- E - Enemy
- BF - Best Friend
- R - Rival
- B - Boss
- Add to this key

Write Draw Journal Craft Here

Character Name:

The Web

Journal Exercise: The Web – Mapping Your Character's Connections

Instructions:
Your character doesn't exist in isolation—the people around them shape who they are, how they act, and how their story unfolds. In this exercise, you'll create a relationship web to see your character's social universe at a glance.

Step 1: Draw the Web
- Write your character's name in the center of the page.
- Around the center, add names of people connected to your character:
  - Family members (parents, siblings, extended family)
  - Friends or allies
  - Mentors, guides, or teachers
  - Rivals, enemies, or antagonists

Step 2: Reflect on Influence
Ask yourself:
- How does each person influence your character?
- Who pushes them to grow or challenges their decisions?
- Who protects them, and who frustrates or opposes them?

Step 3: Label - Use arrows, notes, or symbols to show the type of relationship (supportive, tense, complicated, loving, competitive, etc.)
- S - Stranger (Beginning)
- L - Loath
- ♥ - Love
- FE - Frienemy
- F - Friend
- M - Mom
- D - Dad
- S - Sibling
- E - Enemy
- BF - Best Friend
- R - Rival
- B - Boss
- Add to this key

Write Draw Journal Craft Here

The Web

Character Name:

Journal Exercise: The Web — Mapping Your Character's Connections

Instructions:
Your character doesn't exist in isolation—the people around them shape who they are, how they act, and how their story unfolds. In this exercise, you'll create a relationship web to see your character's social universe at a glance.

Step 1: Draw the Web
- Write your character's name in the center of the page.
- Around the center, add names of people connected to your character:
    - Family members (parents, siblings, extended family)
    - Friends or allies
    - Mentors, guides, or teachers
    - Rivals, enemies, or antagonists

Step 2: Reflect on Influence
Ask yourself:
- How does each person influence your character?
- Who pushes them to grow or challenges their decisions?
- Who protects them, and who frustrates or opposes them?

Step 3: Label - Use arrows, notes, or symbols to show the type of relationship (supportive, tense, complicated, loving, competitive, etc.)
- S - Stranger (Beginning)
- L - Loath
- ♥ - Love
- FE - Frienemy
- F - Friend
- M - Mom
- D - Dad
- S - Sibling
- E - Enemy
- BF - Best Friend
- R - Rival
- B - Boss
- Add to this key

Write Draw Journal Craft Here

Update Your Characters /Attributes

Use this table to capture the key details of each of your characters. Fill in every row with what makes them visually distinct, their personality, quirks, goals, and everyday habits—anything that brings them to life on the page.

	Character Name	Character Name	Character Name
Attribute			
Eye Color			
Hair Color			
Gender			
Race/ Ethnicity			
Height			
Age			
Favorite Color			
Favorite Clothing			
Quirk			
Titles			
Profession			
Speech or Dialect			
Favorite Word(s)			
Country of Origin			

Write Draw Journal Craft Here

THE WEB - TROPES

Prework for Your Story

Now that you've mapped out your web of connections for your protagonist(s), review the list of tropes. Which ones stand out or feel relevant? Identify the tropes that fit naturally with your story and characters—those that can heighten tension, deepen conflict, or add emotional stakes.

TROPE LIST

Considerations

Today's Mood

Write Draw Journal Craft Here

THE MASK

Prework for Your Story

In this section, identify the lie they believe—the false belief or wound that blinds them and blocks growth.

TO-DO LIST

NOTES

Today's Mood

Write Draw Journal Craft Here

Character Name: _____

The Mask – The Lie

Journal Exercise: Digging Deeper into The Lie

Instructions:
1. Every character acts through a lens—a belief that may not be true, but that shapes their choices. Remember: This isn't just backstory—this is the lens through which your character interprets every situation in your story.
2. Dig deeper:
3. Analyze the impact:

What false belief does my character cling to? Write the first answer that comes to mind.

Why do they believe this?

How does this belief protect them? (e.g., keeps them safe, avoids pain)

How does it hold them back? (e.g., prevents growth, blocks love or success)

Observations:

Write Draw Journal Craft Here

Character Name:

The Mask – The Lie

Journal Exercise: Digging Deeper into The Lie
Instructions:
1. Every character acts through a lens—a belief that may not be true, but that shapes their choices. Remember: This isn't just backstory—this is the lens through which your character interprets every situation in your story.
2. Dig deeper:
3. Analyze the impact:

What false belief does my character cling to? Write the first answer that comes to mind.

Why do they believe this?

How does this belief protect them? (e.g., keeps them safe, avoids pain)

How does it hold them back? (e.g., prevents growth, blocks love or success)

Observations:

Write Draw Journal Craft Here

Character Name:

The Mask – The Lie

Journal Exercise: Digging Deeper into The Lie
Instructions:
1. Every character acts through a lens—a belief that may not be true, but that shapes their choices. Remember: This isn't just backstory—this is the lens through which your character interprets every situation in your story.
2. Dig deeper:
3. Analyze the impact:

What false belief does my character cling to? Write the first answer that comes to mind.

Why do they believe this?

How does this belief protect them? (e.g., keeps them safe, avoids pain)

How does it hold them back? (e.g., prevents growth, blocks love or success)

Observations:

Write Draw Journal Craft Here

THE FLAME

Prework for Your Story

In this section, pinpoint wants vs. needs and clear short- and long-term goals that fuel the plot and decisions.

TO-DO LIST

-
-
-
-
-
-
-

NOTES

Today's Mood

Write Draw Journal Craft Here

Character Name: **Goals**

Journal Exercise: Defining Your Character's Goals

Instructions:

Your character's values, beliefs, and desires (from the Heartbeat section) often hint at tangible goals. Goals are what your character actively works toward—they give your story direction, tension, and stakes.

Step 1: Look Back at the Heartbeat Section
- Review the core values, beliefs, and desires you've recorded for your character.
- Identify any aspirations, wishes, or unmet needs that could become goals.

Step 2: Convert Desires into Tangible Goals
- For each potential goal, ask:
   a. Is it tangible? (Can it be clearly seen or measured?)
   b. Is it measurable? (Can you track progress or completion?)
   c. Does it have a timeline? (By when does the character aim to achieve it?)
- Only include goals that meet these criteria.

Goal	Timeline	Measurable: Name Measures or Metrics	Tangible (Y or N)	Notes

Write Draw Journal Craft Here

Character Name: **Goals**

Journal Exercise: Defining Your Character's Goals
Instructions:
Your character's values, beliefs, and desires (from the Heartbeat section) often hint at tangible goals. Goals are what your character actively works toward—they give your story direction, tension, and stakes.

Step 1: Look Back at the Heartbeat Section
- Review the core values, beliefs, and desires you've recorded for your character.
- Identify any aspirations, wishes, or unmet needs that could become goals.

Step 2: Convert Desires into Tangible Goals
- For each potential goal, ask:
    a. Is it tangible? (Can it be clearly seen or measured?)
    b. Is it measurable? (Can you track progress or completion?)
    c. Does it have a timeline? (By when does the character aim to achieve it?)
- Only include goals that meet these criteria.

Goal	Timeline	Measurable: Name Measures or Metrics	Tangible (Y or N)	Notes

Write Draw Journal Craft Here

Character Name: **Goals**

Journal Exercise: Defining Your Character's Goals

Instructions:

Your character's values, beliefs, and desires (from the Heartbeat section) often hint at tangible goals. Goals are what your character actively works toward—they give your story direction, tension, and stakes.

Step 1: Look Back at the Heartbeat Section
- Review the core values, beliefs, and desires you've recorded for your character.
- Identify any aspirations, wishes, or unmet needs that could become goals.

Step 2: Convert Desires into Tangible Goals
- For each potential goal, ask:
    a. Is it tangible? (Can it be clearly seen or measured?)
    b. Is it measurable? (Can you track progress or completion?)
    c. Does it have a timeline? (By when does the character aim to achieve it?)
- Only include goals that meet these criteria.

Goal	Timeline	Measurable: Name Measures or Metrics	Tangible (Y or N)	Notes

Write Draw Journal Craft Here

THE STORM

Prework for Your Story

In this section, write out the external barriers and internal doubts that test them—failures that reveal true character.

Every character faces storms—moments that test their resolve, expose their weaknesses, and block their progress. These can be external obstacles (other people, systems, or physical barriers) or internal conflicts (fears, doubts, or lies they believe).

Be specific when brainstorming lists—storms are what create tension and growth in your story.

TO-DO LIST

NOTES

Today's Mood

Write Draw Journal Craft Here

External Vs. Internal

Character Name:

Journal Exercise: The Storm — Obstacles & Inner Conflict
Instructions:
Step 1: Identify External Obstacles
- Who or what stands in your character's way?
- Is it a rival, a law, a lack of resources, or a dangerous environment?

Step 2: Identify Internal Conflicts
- What fears, insecurities, or false beliefs sabotage them?
- What past wounds keep resurfacing?

Obstacle / Conflict	Ext or Int	Why It Matters	How It Challenges the Character	Possible Outcome

Observations:

Write Draw Journal Craft Here

Character Name:

External Vs. Internal

Journal Exercise: The Storm — Obstacles & Inner Conflict

Instructions:

Step 1: Identify External Obstacles
- Who or what stands in your character's way?
- Is it a rival, a law, a lack of resources, or a dangerous environment?

Step 2: Identify Internal Conflicts
- What fears, insecurities, or false beliefs sabotage them?
- What past wounds keep resurfacing?

Obstacle / Conflict	Ext or Int	Why It Matters	How It Challenges the Character	Possible Outcome

Observations:

Write Draw Journal Craft Here

THE MIRROR

Prework for Your Story

In this section, balance talents with weaknesses so the character is capable yet vulnerable and relatable.

Every strength casts a shadow. Courage can look like recklessness. Intelligence can lead to arrogance. Kindness can make someone vulnerable to being used. The most compelling characters hold both light and shadow.

In the brainstorming exercise, you'll map your character's strengths alongside their flaws, and notice how one often mirrors the other.

TO-DO LIST

NOTES

Today's Mood

Write Draw Journal Craft Here

Character Name:

Strengths & Weaknesses

Journal Exercise: Digging Deeper into Motivations and Story Problems
Instructions:
List Strengths: What skills, traits, or talents make your character capable, admirable, or unique? Think both practical (good fighter, clever strategist) and personal (loyal friend, quick thinker).
List Flaws: Where do they stumble? What blind spots, habits, or weaknesses sabotage them? Which flaws are connected to their strengths?

Strengths

Weaknesses

Observations:

Write Draw Journal Craft Here

Character Name:

Strengths & Weaknesses

Journal Exercise: Digging Deeper into Motivations and Story Problems

Instructions:

List Strengths: What skills, traits, or talents make your character capable, admirable, or unique? Think both practical (good fighter, clever strategist) and personal (loyal friend, quick thinker).

List Flaws: Where do they stumble? What blind spots, habits, or weaknesses sabotage them? Which flaws are connected to their strengths?

Strengths

Weaknesses

Observations:

Write Draw Journal Craft Here

THE ARC

Prework for Your Story

In this section, map the turning points and choices that produce measurable growth or arrest their evolution and change experienced throughout the story.

Every strong story follows a character through change. The arc is how your character grows—or resists growth—over the course of the story. Use the story curve to map how your character's goals, beliefs, relationships, and core lie evolve and change at point of the story: the beginning, the middle, and the end.

Think in three acts:
- Beginning: Who they are before the storm.
- Middle: How pressure tests them and forces hard choices.
- End: Who they've become after facing conflict and truth.

TO-DO LIST

NOTES

Today's Mood

Write Draw Journal Craft Here

Romancing the Beat	
Introduce Hero/Heroine (Phase 1: Set Up) - Introduce the first protagonist, their ordinary life, internal struggles, external goals, and hint at what they need to grow.	
Meet Cute (Phase 1: Set Up) - The first encounter between the two protagonists, sparked by circumstance, chance, or conflict; hints at attraction and tension.	
Introduce H2 (Phase 1: Set Up) - Introduce the second protagonist in their ordinary life, showing their desires, flaws, and goals.	
No Way 1 (Phase 1: Set Up) - H1 voices their reason for avoiding love, particularly with H2, establishing initial resistance.	
Adhesion (Phase 1: Set Up) - An event forces the protagonists together, raising stakes and sparking attraction despite conflict.	
No Way 2 (Phase 2: Falling in Love) - H1 reasserts resistance; internal needs clash with external goals, keeping the romance at bay.	
Inkling of Desire (Phase 2: Falling in Love) - Characters begin admitting feelings; false beliefs are challenged.	
Deepening Desire (Phase 2: Falling in Love) - Emotional connection strengthens; protagonists reveal true selves, further eroding resistance.	

Story Arcs

Think How Goals, Beliefs, Relationships, and the Lie Change as the Story Progresses

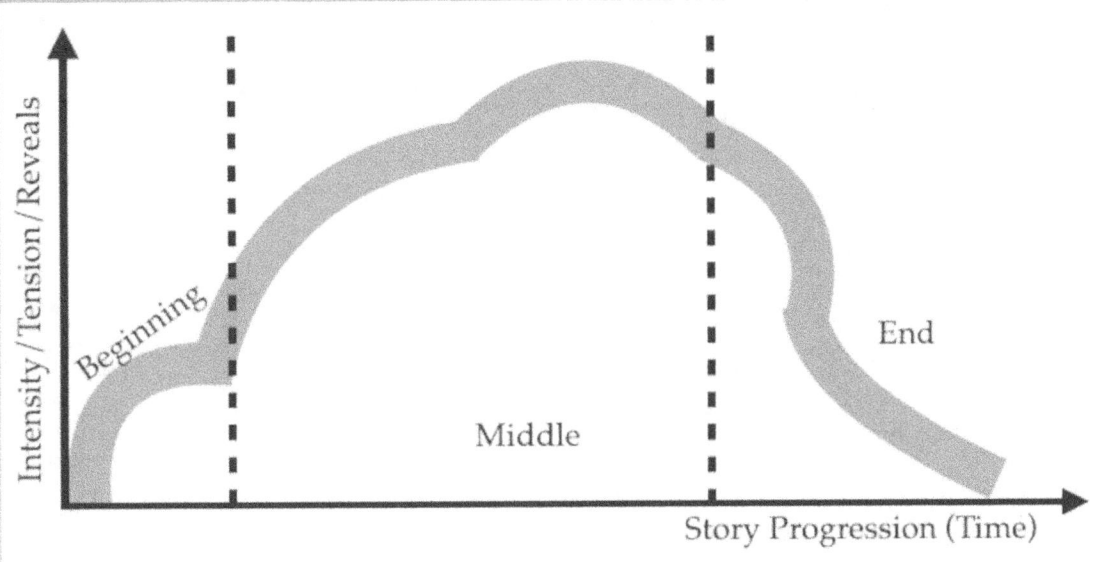

Stage	Goals	Beliefs	Relationships	The Lie They Believe
Beginning	What do they want at the start?	What do they believe is true about themselves or the world?	Who matters most to them at the start?	What false belief limits them?
Middle	How do their goals shift under pressure?	What beliefs get challenged or shaken?	Which relationships grow, break, or surprise them?	How does the lie start to crack (or strengthen)?
End	What do they want now? Did they achieve their original goal?	What truth or new belief replaces the old one?	Who's still with them—and how has trust/love changed?	How do they face or overcome the lie?

Write Draw Journal Craft Here

Write Draw Journal Craft Here

Romancing the Beat	
Maybe This Could Work (Phase 2: Falling in Love) - Protagonists question prior resistance, tension grows between feelings and goals.	
Midpoint of Love (Phase 2: Falling in Love) - A false high; protagonists glimpse the possibility of love while balancing goals and desires.	
Inkling of Doubt (Phase 3: Retreating From Love) - Old doubts and false beliefs return; characters begin pulling back.	
Deepening Doubt (Phase 3: Retreating From Love) - Intimacy continues but seeds of doubt affect the relationship.	
Retreat Beat (Phase 3: Retreating From Love) - Trust falters; characters articulate fears and protect their hearts.	
Shields Up (Phase 3: Retreating From Love) - Worst-case scenario; prior "No Way" fears seem validated, relationship breaks down.	
Break Up (Phase 3: Retreating From Love) - Relationship ends; protagonists cling to false beliefs or fears.	

Write Draw Journal Craft Here

Story Arcs

Character:

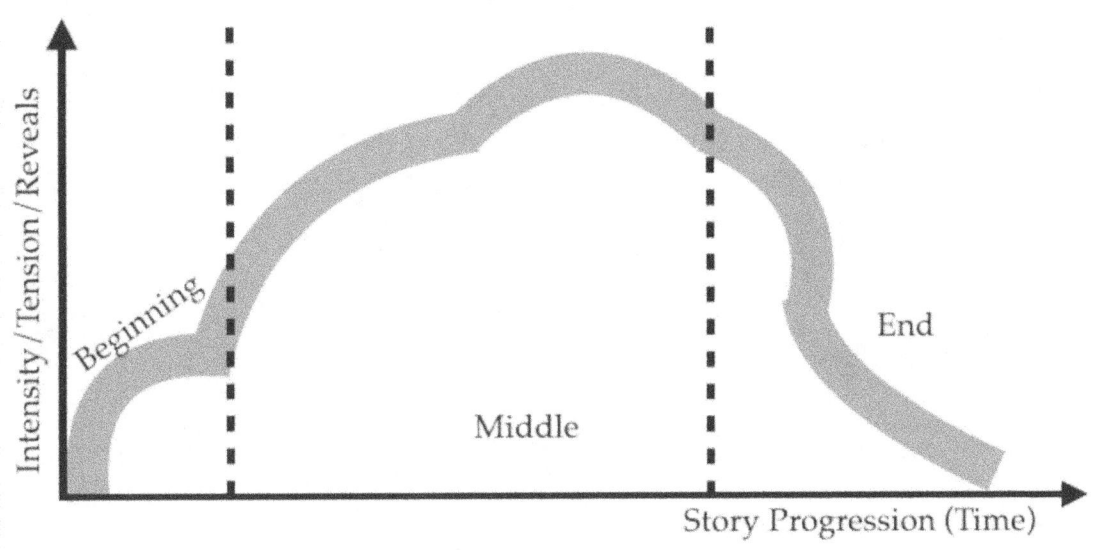

Beginning:

Middle:

End:

Write Draw Journal Craft Here

Write Draw Journal Craft Here

Romancing the Beat	
Dark Night (Phase 4: Fighting for Love) – "What have I done?" moment; reflection on past choices and lingering feelings.	
Wake Up (Phase 4: Fighting for Love) – Protagonist chooses love over fear; begins actively fighting for the relationship.	
Grand Gesture (Phase 4: Fighting for Love) – A dramatic act to prove commitment and overcome obstacles to love.	
What Wholehearted Looks Like (Phase 4: Fighting for Love) – Characters show personal growth and emotional transformation; relationship solidifies.	
Epilogue (Phase 4: Fighting for Love) – Return to the ordinary world, showing the protagonists' transformed selves and happy resolution.	

Write Draw Journal Craft Here

Story Arcs

Character:

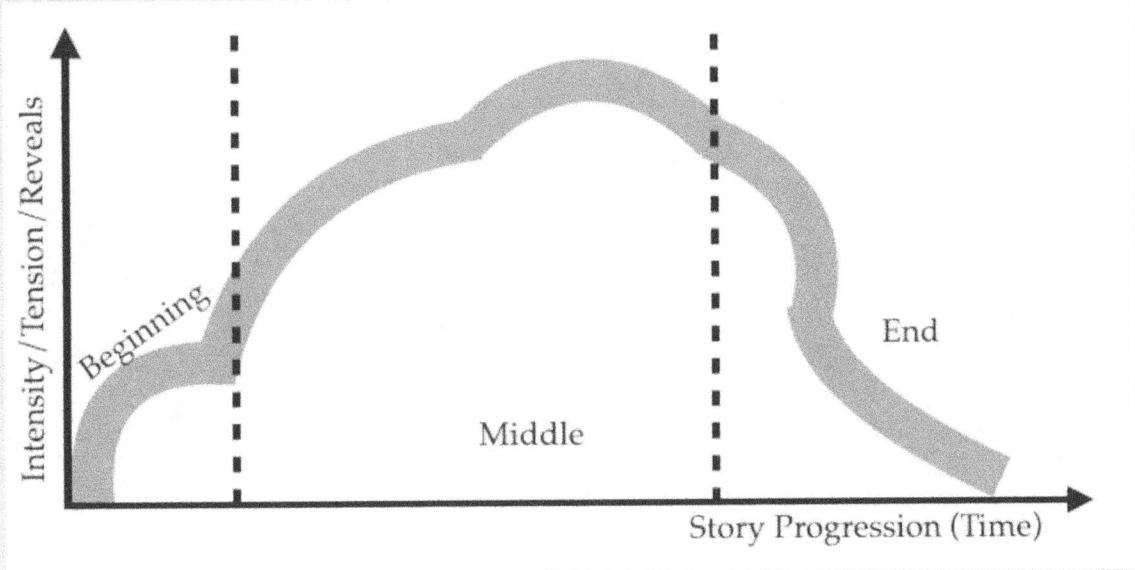

Beginning:

Middle:

End:

Write Draw Journal Craft Here

Write Draw Journal Craft Here

7 Romantic Comedy Beats	
The Chemical Equation (Setup) - Introduces the protagonist's internal and external conflicts and their ordinary world.	
Meet Cute (The Catalyst / Inciting Incident) - The first meeting of the protagonist and love interest, sparking conflict and/or attraction.	
A Sexy Complication (Turning Point 1) - A development that raises stakes and shows the characters at cross-purposes, building romantic tension.	
The Hook (Midpoint) - A situation binds the characters together, deepening connection while challenging beliefs or goals.	
Swivel (Turning Point 2) - The relationship's stakes peak; the romance conflicts with external goals, leading to a pivotal choice.	
Dark Moment (Crisis / Climax) - The "all is lost" moment; the relationship and/or the protagonist's goals seem doomed.	
Joyful Defeat (Resolution) - The protagonist(s) reconcile, resolve internal and external conflicts, and commit to love, often with some personal sacrifice.	

Write Draw Journal Craft Here

Story Arcs

Character:

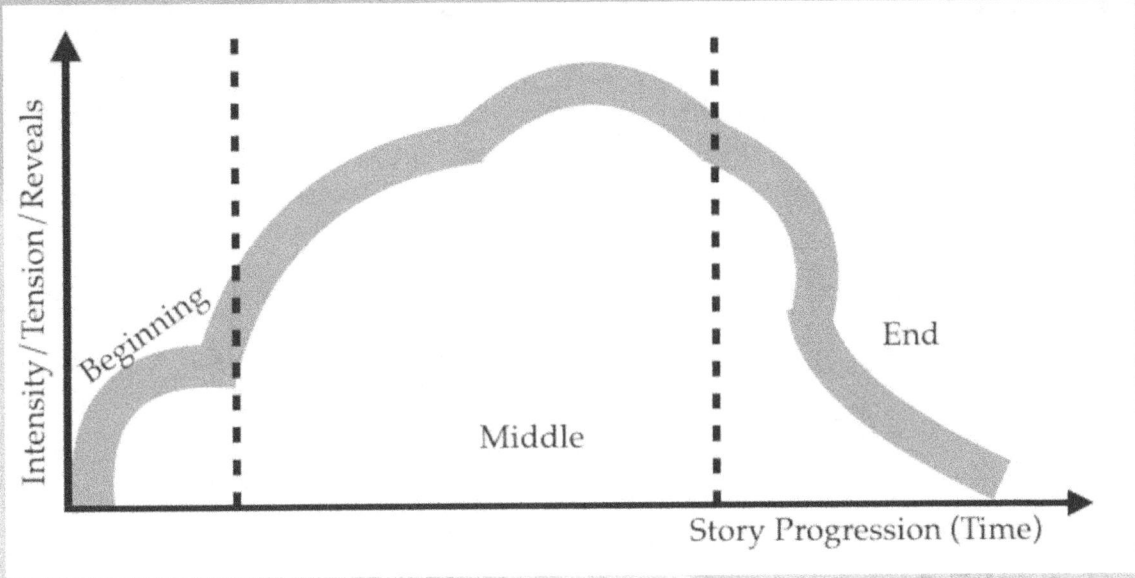

Beginning:

Middle:

End:

Write Draw Journal Craft Here

Write Draw Journal Craft Here

Romantasy Beats	
World & Protagonist Setup - H1 meets H2 (or is forced into proximity) through some fantasy event (e.g., curse, magical accident, alliance necessity). The catalyst disturbs both personal and world status quo.	
Meet of Love & Catalyst - H1 meets H2 (or is forced into proximity) through some fantasy event (e.g., curse, magical accident, alliance necessity). The catalyst disturbs both personal and world status quo.	
First Resistance / "No Way"- H1 resists romance due to internal beliefs/fears, responsibilities, or because romance conflicts with fantasy duty (e.g., prophecy states love must be sacrificed).	
Forced Cooperation / World Stakes Raise -External fantasy plot pushes them together—maybe to solve a magical problem, fight a common enemy, or undertake a quest. Their romantic chemistry starts under duress.	
Deepening Connection + Fantasy Conflict - They share vulnerability; fantasy stakes magnify (e.g. one's magic is dangerous or unstable). Conflict between what they want romantically vs what the world demands.	
Midpoint / False Hope A turning point where both romance & fantasy goals seem aligned—maybe a victory or breakthrough that suggests they might have both love and save the world.	
Betrayal or Dark Revelation Something is revealed about fantasy world rules, past betrayals, or magical curses that threatens trust or loyalty. The romantic relationship is tested heavily.	

Write Draw Journal Craft Here

Story Arcs

Character (3):

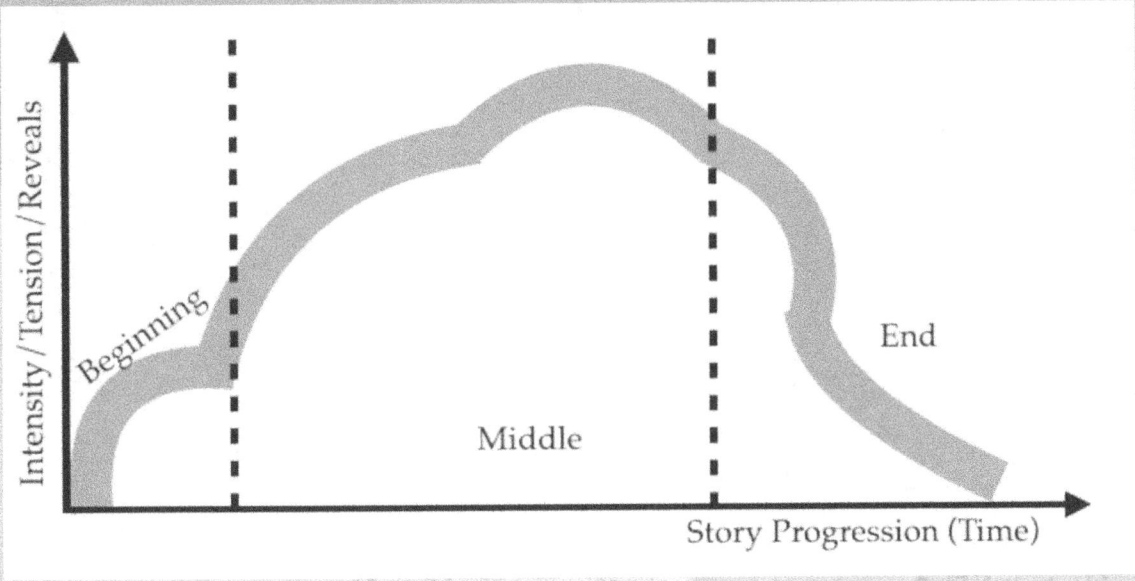

Beginning:

Middle:

End:

Write Draw Journal Craft Here

THE WORLD

Prework for Your Story

In this section, list factors of the environment--culture, geography (the sky above, the land below), class, and time period (Regency, Gilded Age, Victorian, etc.) shape identity, perspective, and a character's options and opportunities.

Aspect of the World	How It Shapes Daily Life	Impact on Character
Geography/ Climate	Example: Harsh winters make survival difficult	Builds resilience and caution
Culture/ Traditions	Example: Community celebrates storytelling	Character values oral history
Class/ Wealth	Example: Born into poverty	Struggles with ambition vs. shame
Politics/ Power	Example: Corrupt monarchy rules	Character distrusts authority
Religion/ Belief Systems	Example: Strong emphasis on ritual	Character feels trapped or inspired

TO-DO LIST

NOTES

Today's Mood

Write Draw Journal Craft Here

The World

Global Location:

Journal Exercise: Building the World
Instructions:
Map the world around them, filling out the table below to capture how the world influences your character? Build one for each significant location. Start global. Then do local - homes, office, etc.

City, Country, Kingdom

Climate

Customs

Geography

Cultural Beliefs

Year or Time

Observations:

Write Draw Journal Craft Here

The World

Local Location:

Journal Exercise: Building the World
Instructions:
Map the world around them, filling out the table below to capture how the world influences your character? Build one for each significant location. Start global. Then do local - homes, office, etc.

City	House or Room Description

House Practices	Geography – City Streets, etc.

Unusual	Weather

Observations:

Write Draw Journal Craft Here

Character Name:

The World

Journal Exercise: Building the World
Instructions:
Map the world around them, filling out the table below to capture how the world influences your character? Build one for each significant location. Start global. Then do local - homes, office, etc.

City

Favorite Place

Favorite Activity

Geography - City Streets, etc.

Job

Favorite Weather

Observations:

Write Draw Journal Craft Here

Character Name: # The World

Journal Exercise: Building the World
Instructions:
Map the world around them, filling out the table below to capture how the world influences your character? Build one for each significant location. Start global. Then do local - homes, office, etc.

City	Favorite Place

Favorite Activity	Geography - City Streets, etc.

Job	Favorite Weather

Observations:

Write Draw Journal Craft Here

The World

Character Name:

Journal Exercise: Building the World
Instructions:
Map the world around them, filling out the table below to capture how the world influences your character? Build one for each significant location. Start global. Then do local - homes, office, etc.

City

Favorite Place

Favorite Activity

Geography - City Streets, etc.

Job

Favorite Weather

Observations:

Write Draw Journal Craft Here

THE FULL CIRCLE

Prework for Your Story

In this section, complete the character's arc with an earned resolution that shows who they became and why it matters.

TO-DO LIST

- ....
- ....
- ....
- ....
- ....
- ....
- ....

NOTES

....
....
....
....
....
....
....
....
....

Today's Mood

Write Draw Journal Craft Here

Character Name:

The Pre – Synopsis 1

Journal Exercise: The Full Circle — Writing Your Character Synopsis
Instructions:
Now it's time to bring everything together. Using your notes from previous sections, write a short synopsis that captures your character's journey from beginning to end. This synopsis should highlight who they are, what they want, what stands in their way, and how they change.

Who is your character at the beginning (ordinary life, Spark)?

What do they believe (Heartbeat), and what lie do they carry (Mask)?

What do they want most (Flame)?

Who is in their corner or in their way (Web)?

Notes:

Write Draw Journal Craft Here

Character Name:

The Pre – Synopsis 2

Journal Exercise: The Full Circle — Writing Your Character Synopsis
Instructions:
Now it's time to bring everything together. Using your notes from previous sections, write a short synopsis that captures your character's journey from beginning to end. This synopsis should highlight who they are, what they want, what stands in their way, and how they change.

What challenges or conflicts test them (Storm)?

How do their strengths and flaws (Mirror) drive success or mistakes?

What critical moment forces them to grow (Arc)?

Notes:

Write Draw Journal Craft Here

Character Name:

The Pre – Synopsis 3

Journal Exercise: The Full Circle — Writing Your Character Synopsis
Instructions:
Now it's time to bring everything together. Using your notes from previous sections, write a short synopsis that captures your character's journey from beginning to end. This synopsis should highlight who they are, what they want, what stands in their way, and how they change.

Where does the journey leave them?

What truth replaces their lie?

How have their goals, beliefs, and relationships changed?

What final choice defines them?

Notes:

Write Draw Journal Craft Here

Mini Synopsis

Using your answers, combine everything into a 1-3 paragraph character synopsis. Write it in third person, like a back-cover blurb.

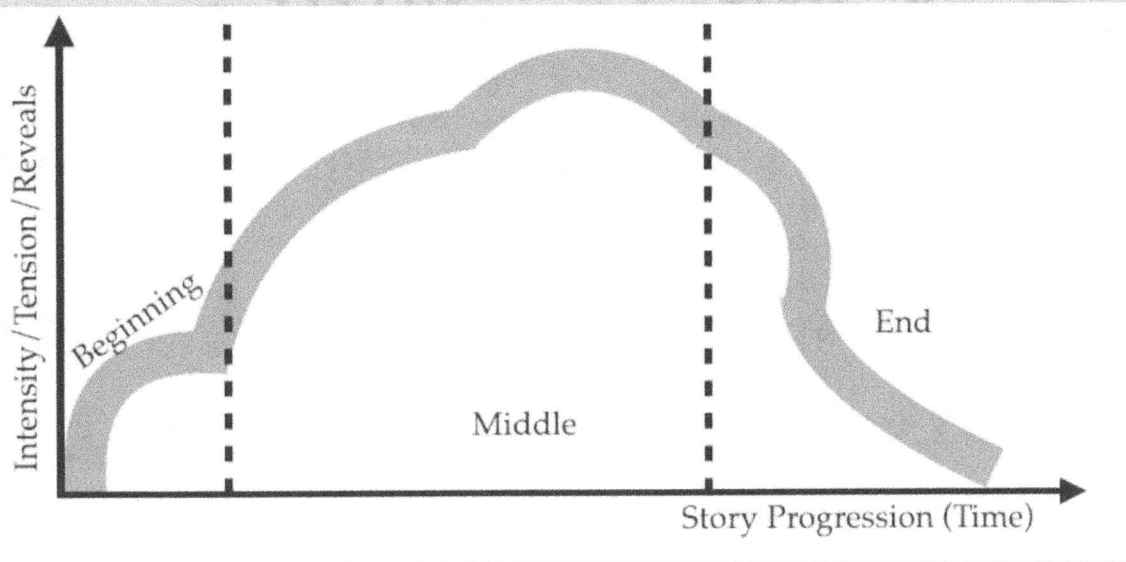

Beginning:

Write Draw Journal Craft Here

Mini Synopsis

Using your answers, combine everything into a 1-3 paragraph character synopsis. Write it in third person, like a back-cover blurb.

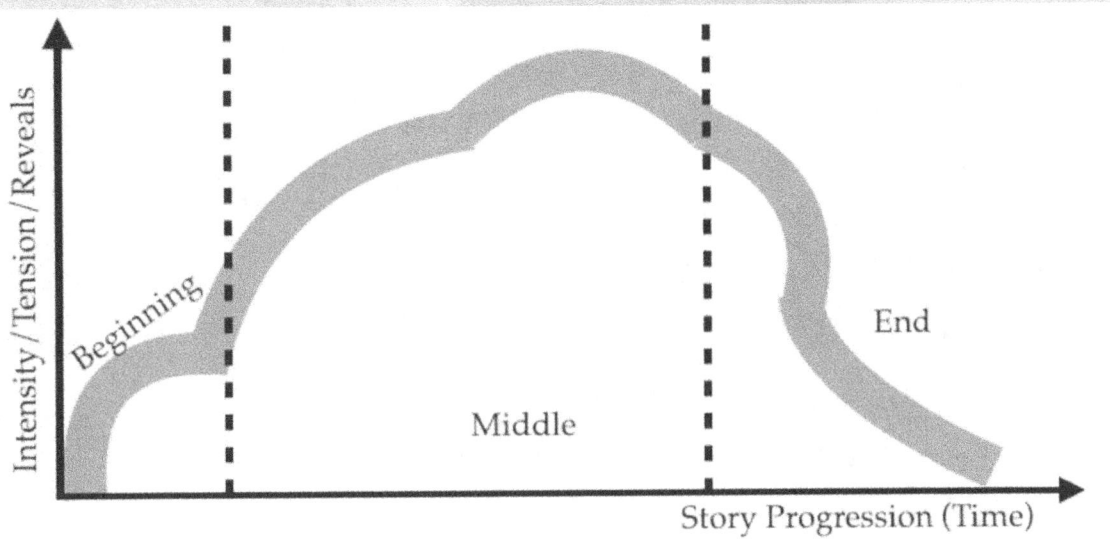

Middle:

Write Draw Journal Craft Here

Mini Synopsis

Using your answers, combine everything into a 1-3 paragraph character synopsis. Write it in third person, like a back-cover blurb.

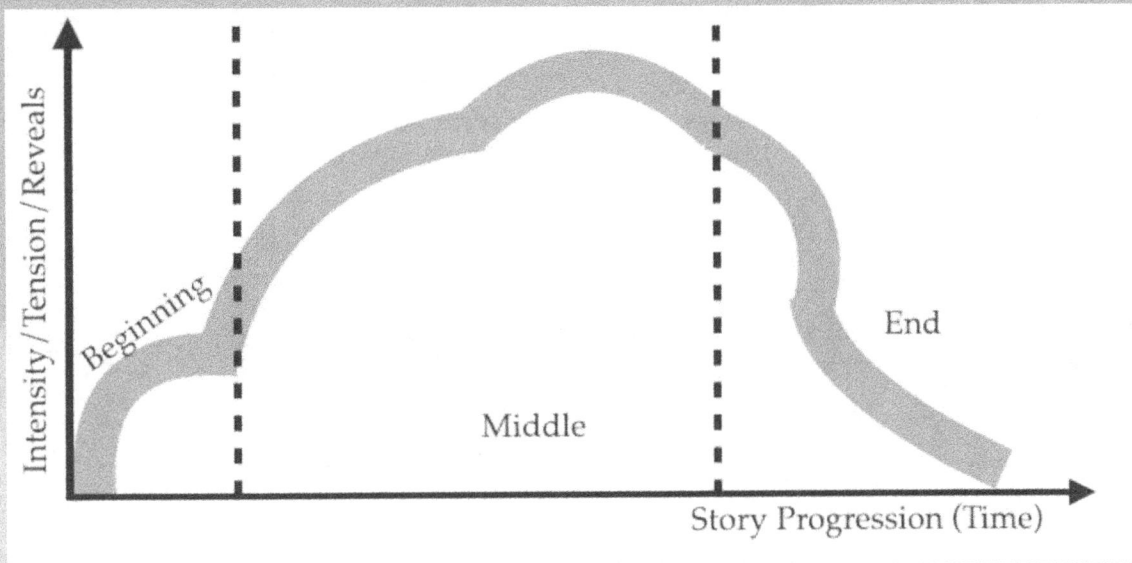

End:

Write Draw Journal Craft Here

Romancing the Beat

Using your answers, answer the questions for Romancing the Beat or 7 Romantic Comedy Beats

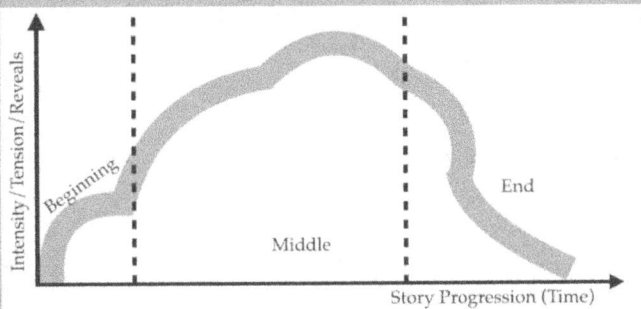

Romancing the Beat	
Introduce Hero/Heroine (Phase 1: Set Up) - Introduce the first protagonist, their ordinary life, internal struggles, external goals, and hint at what they need to grow.	
Meet Cute (Phase 1: Set Up) - The first encounter between the two protagonists, sparked by circumstance, chance, or conflict; hints at attraction and tension.	
Introduce H2 (Phase 1: Set Up) - Introduce the second protagonist in their ordinary life, showing their desires, flaws, and goals.	
No Way 1 (Phase 1: Set Up) - H1 voices their reason for avoiding love, particularly with H2, establishing initial resistance.	
Adhesion (Phase 1: Set Up) - An event forces the protagonists together, raising stakes and sparking attraction despite conflict.	
No Way 2 (Phase 2: Falling in Love) - H1 reasserts resistance; internal needs clash with external goals, keeping the romance at bay.	
Inkling of Desire (Phase 2: Falling in Love) - Characters begin admitting feelings; false beliefs are challenged.	
Deepening Desire (Phase 2: Falling in Love) - Emotional connection strengthens; protagonists reveal true selves, further eroding resistance.	

Write Draw Journal Craft Here

Romancing the Beat

Using your answers, answer the questions for Romancing the Beat or 7 Romantic Comedy Beats

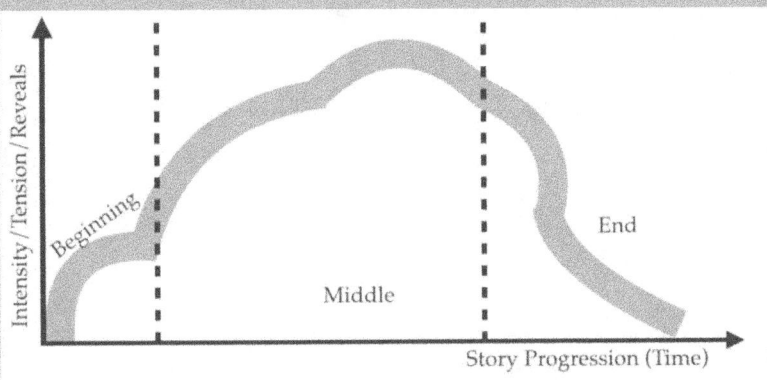

Romancing the Beat	
Maybe This Could Work (Phase 2: Falling in Love) - Protagonists question prior resistance, tension grows between feelings and goals.	
Midpoint of Love (Phase 2: Falling in Love) - A false high; protagonists glimpse the possibility of love while balancing goals and desires.	
Inkling of Doubt (Phase 3: Retreating From Love) - Old doubts and false beliefs return; characters begin pulling back.	
Deepening Doubt (Phase 3: Retreating From Love) - Intimacy continues but seeds of doubt affect the relationship.	
Retreat Beat (Phase 3: Retreating From Love) - Trust falters; characters articulate fears and protect their hearts.	
Shields Up (Phase 3: Retreating From Love) - Worst-case scenario; prior "No Way" fears seem validated, relationship breaks down.	
Break Up (Phase 3: Retreating From Love) - Relationship ends; protagonists cling to false beliefs or fears.	

Write Draw Journal Craft Here

Romancing the Beat

Using your answers, answer the questions for Romancing the Beat or 7 Romantic Comedy Beats

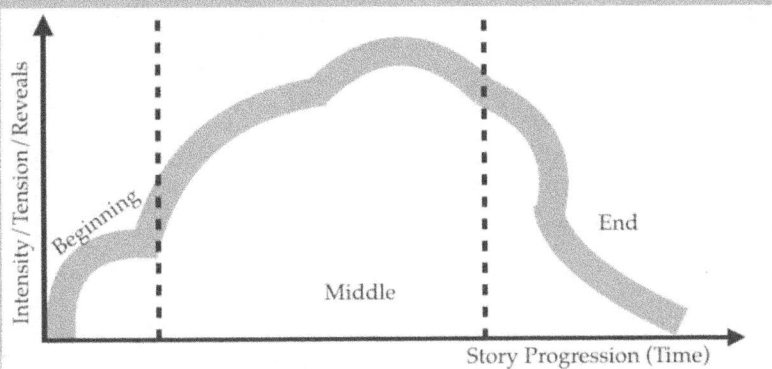

Romancing the Beat	
Dark Night (Phase 4: Fighting for Love) – "What have I done?" moment; reflection on past choices and lingering feelings.	
Wake Up (Phase 4: Fighting for Love) – Protagonist chooses love over fear; begins actively fighting for the relationship.	
Grand Gesture (Phase 4: Fighting for Love) – A dramatic act to prove commitment and overcome obstacles to love.	
What Wholehearted Looks Like (Phase 4: Fighting for Love) – Characters show personal growth and emotional transformation; relationship solidifies.	
Epilogue (Phase 4: Fighting for Love) – Return to the ordinary world, showing the protagonists' transformed selves and happy resolution.	

Write Draw Journal Craft Here

7 Romantic Comedy Beats

Using your answers, answer the questions for Romancing the Beat or 7 Romantic Comedy Beats

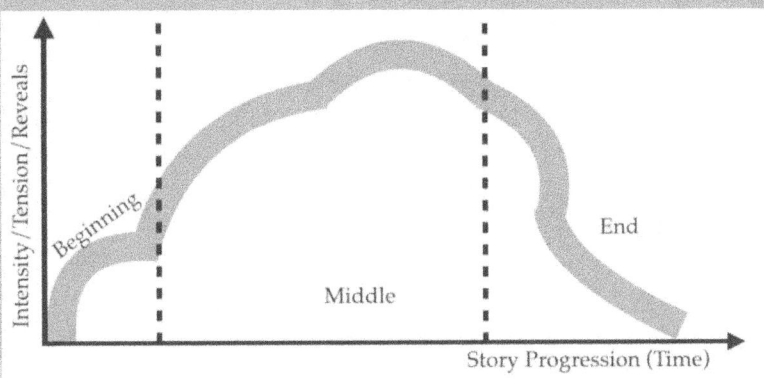

7 Romantic Comedy Beats	
The Chemical Equation (Setup) - Introduces the protagonist's internal and external conflicts and their ordinary world.	
Meet Cute (The Catalyst / Inciting Incident) - The first meeting of the protagonist and love interest, sparking conflict and/or attraction.	
A Sexy Complication (Turning Point 1) - A development that raises stakes and shows the characters at cross-purposes, building romantic tension.	
The Hook (Midpoint) - A situation binds the characters together, deepening connection while challenging beliefs or goals.	
Swivel (Turning Point 2) - The relationship's stakes peak; the romance conflicts with external goals, leading to a pivotal choice.	
Dark Moment (Crisis / Climax) - The "all is lost" moment; the relationship and/or the protagonist's goals seem doomed.	
Joyful Defeat (Resolution) - The protagonist(s) reconcile, resolve internal and external conflicts, and commit to love, often with some personal sacrifice.	

Write Draw Journal Craft Here

Romantasy Beats

Using your answers, build the Romantasy Beats.

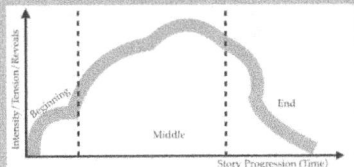

Romantasy Beats	
World & Protagonist Setup – H1 meets H2 (or is forced into proximity) through some fantasy event (e.g., curse, magical accident, alliance necessity). The catalyst disturbs both personal and world status quo.	
Meet of Love & Catalyst – H1 meets H2 (or is forced into proximity) through some fantasy event (e.g., curse, magical accident, alliance necessity). The catalyst disturbs both personal and world status quo.	
First Resistance / "No Way"– H1 resists romance due to internal beliefs/fears, responsibilities, or because romance conflicts with fantasy duty (e.g., prophecy states love must be sacrificed).	
Forced Cooperation / World Stakes Raise –External fantasy plot pushes them together—maybe to solve a magical problem, fight a common enemy, or undertake a quest. Their romantic chemistry starts under duress.	
Deepening Connection + Fantasy Conflict – They share vulnerability; fantasy stakes magnify (e.g. one's magic is dangerous or unstable). Conflict between what they want romantically vs what the world demands.	
Midpoint / False Hope A turning point where both romance & fantasy goals seem aligned—maybe a victory or breakthrough that suggests they might have both love and save the world.	
Betrayal or Dark Revelation Something is revealed about fantasy world rules, past betrayals, or magical curses that threatens trust or loyalty. The romantic relationship is tested heavily.	

Write Draw Journal Craft Here

WRITING GOALS

Prework for Your Story

In this section, you've done the prework—now it's time to shift gears and set clear weekly writing goals that keep your story moving forward.

Writing on a consistent basis is the way to finish your story!

	100 Per Day	500 Per Day	1000 Per Week
Novella ~ 30,000	Year	2 Months	6 Months
Category ~ 50,000	1.5 Year	4 Months	1 Year
Novel ~ 75,000	2 Years	5 Months	18 Months

TO-DO LIST

☐ ....
☐ ....
☐ ....
☐ ....
☐ ....
☐ ....
☐ ....

NOTES

Today's Mood

Write Draw Journal Craft Here

Writing Goals

Steady Writing Wins!

What is your commitment: (Goals have timelines or deadlines.

Name:

Word Count:

Date:

Daily or Weekly Writing Goals for Your Project:

Notes or Commitments:

Write Draw Journal Craft Here

Writing Goals

Week: _____

Mood/Emotion Tracker

○ ○ ○ ○ ○
SAD STABLE WIP HAPPY JOYFUL
⟵⟶

Doodle Space:

Writing Goals for Your Project

Writing Goals for The Week:

What I'm Proud of This Week:

Emotional Writing Suggestions

SAD
- Doodle or sketch something comforting
- Write down one small thing that went well today
- Work on your character's low points / conflict scenes

STABLE
- Doodle Happy Thoughts
- Read over your latest sketch or scene
- Freewrite 100 words (no editing)

WIP
- Doodle or brainstorm ideas
- Affirm "I am a work in progress"
- Freewrite 500 words or rework a scene

HAPPY
- Doodle your character's happy place
- Write for 60 minutes (split into 20-min sessions with breaks)
- Optional: Edit or expand on scenes

JOYFUL
- Doodle your personal happy place or story idea
- Write for 60–90 minutes (multiple sessions)
- Optional: start a second writing session
- Reflect or plan next steps

Write Draw Journal Craft Here

Writing Goals

Week: _____

Mood/Emotion Tracker

○ ○ ○ ○ ○
SAD STABLE WIP HAPPY JOYFUL
         ↔

Doodle Space:

Writing Goals for Your Project

Writing Goals for The Week:

What I'm Proud of This Week:

Emotional Writing Suggestions

SAD
- Doodle or sketch something comforting
- Write down one small thing that went well today
- Work on your character's low points / conflict scenes

STABLE
- Doodle Happy Thoughts
- Read over your latest sketch or scene
- Freewrite 100 words (no editing)

WIP
- Doodle or brainstorm ideas
- Affirm "I am a work in progress"
- Freewrite 500 words or rework a scene

HAPPY
- Doodle your character's happy place
- Write for 60 minutes (split into 20-min sessions with breaks)
- Optional: Edit or expand on scenes

JOYFUL
- Doodle your personal happy place or story idea
- Write for 60–90 minutes (multiple sessions)
- Optional: start a second writing session
- Reflect or plan next steps

Write Draw Journal Craft Here

Writing Goals

Week: _____

Mood/Emotion Tracker

◯ ◯ ◯ ◯ ◯
SAD STABLE WIP HAPPY JOYFUL
         ⟷

Doodle Space:

Writing Goals for Your Project

Writing Goals for The Week:

What I'm Proud of This Week:

Emotional Writing Suggestions

SAD
- Doodle or sketch something comforting
- Write down one small thing that went well today
- Work on your character's low points / conflict scenes

STABLE
- Doodle Happy Thoughts
- Read over your latest sketch or scene
- Freewrite 100 words (no editing)

WIP
- Doodle or brainstorm ideas
- Affirm "I am a work in progress"
- Freewrite 500 words or rework a scene

HAPPY
- Doodle your character's happy place
- Write for 60 minutes (split into 20-min sessions with breaks)
- Optional: Edit or expand on scenes

JOYFUL
- Doodle your personal happy place or story idea
- Write for 60–90 minutes (multiple sessions)
- Optional: start a second writing session
- Reflect or plan next steps

Write Draw Journal Craft Here

Writing Goals

Week: _____

Mood/Emotion Tracker

○ ○ ○ ○ ○
SAD STABLE WIP HAPPY JOYFUL
　　　　　↔

Doodle Space:

Writing Goals for Your Project

Writing Goals for The Week:

What I'm Proud of This Week:

Emotional Writing Suggestions

SAD
- Doodle or sketch something comforting
- Write down one small thing that went well today
- Work on your character's low points / conflict scenes

STABLE
- Doodle Happy Thoughts
- Read over your latest sketch or scene
- Freewrite 100 words (no editing)

WIP
- Doodle or brainstorm ideas
- Affirm "I am a work in progress"
- Freewrite 500 words or rework a scene

HAPPY
- Doodle your character's happy place
- Write for 60 minutes (split into 20-min sessions with breaks)
- Optional: Edit or expand on scenes

JOYFUL
- Doodle your personal happy place or story idea
- Write for 60–90 minutes (multiple sessions)
- Optional: start a second writing session
- Reflect or plan next steps

Write Draw Journal Craft Here

Writing Goals

Week: _____

Mood/Emotion Tracker

○ ○ ○ ○ ○
SAD STABLE WIP HAPPY JOYFUL
              ↔

Doodle Space:

Writing Goals for Your Project

Writing Goals for The Week:

Emotional Writing Suggestions

SAD
- Doodle or sketch something comforting
- Write down one small thing that went well today
- Work on your character's low points / conflict scenes

STABLE
- Doodle Happy Thoughts
- Read over your latest sketch or scene
- Freewrite 100 words (no editing)

WIP
- Doodle or brainstorm ideas
- Affirm "I am a work in progress"
- Freewrite 500 words or rework a scene

HAPPY
- Doodle your character's happy place
- Write for 60 minutes (split into 20-min sessions with breaks)
- Optional: Edit or expand on scenes

JOYFUL
- Doodle your personal happy place or story idea
- Write for 60–90 minutes (multiple sessions)
- Optional: start a second writing session
- Reflect or plan next steps

What I'm Proud of This Week:

Write Draw Journal Craft Here

Writing Goals

Week: _____

Mood/Emotion Tracker

○ ○ ○ ○ ○
SAD STABLE WIP HAPPY JOYFUL
⟷

Doodle Space:

Writing Goals for Your Project

Writing Goals for The Week:

What I'm Proud of This Week:

Emotional Writing Suggestions

SAD
- Doodle or sketch something comforting
- Write down one small thing that went well today
- Work on your character's low points / conflict scenes

STABLE
- Doodle Happy Thoughts
- Read over your latest sketch or scene
- Freewrite 100 words (no editing)

WIP
- Doodle or brainstorm ideas
- Affirm "I am a work in progress"
- Freewrite 500 words or rework a scene

HAPPY
- Doodle your character's happy place
- Write for 60 minutes (split into 20-min sessions with breaks)
- Optional: Edit or expand on scenes

JOYFUL
- Doodle your personal happy place or story idea
- Write for 60–90 minutes (multiple sessions)
- Optional: start a second writing session
- Reflect or plan next steps

Write Draw Journal Craft Here

Writing Goals

Week: _____

Mood/Emotion Tracker

○ ○ ○ ○ ○
SAD STABLE WIP HAPPY JOYFUL
         ⟵⟶

Doodle Space:

Writing Goals for Your Project

Writing Goals for The Week:

What I'm Proud of This Week:

Emotional Writing Suggestions

SAD
- Doodle or sketch something comforting
- Write down one small thing that went well today
- Work on your character's low points / conflict scenes

STABLE
- Doodle Happy Thoughts
- Read over your latest sketch or scene
- Freewrite 100 words (no editing)

WIP
- Doodle or brainstorm ideas
- Affirm "I am a work in progress"
- Freewrite 500 words or rework a scene

HAPPY
- Doodle your character's happy place
- Write for 60 minutes (split into 20-min sessions with breaks)
- Optional: Edit or expand on scenes

JOYFUL
- Doodle your personal happy place or story idea
- Write for 60–90 minutes (multiple sessions)
- Optional: start a second writing session
- Reflect or plan next steps

Write Draw Journal Craft Here

Writing Goals

Week: _____

Mood/Emotion Tracker

○ ○ ○ ○ ○
SAD STABLE WIP ⟷ HAPPY JOYFUL

Doodle Space:

Writing Goals for Your Project

Writing Goals for The Week:

What I'm Proud of This Week:

Emotional Writing Suggestions

SAD
- Doodle or sketch something comforting
- Write down one small thing that went well today
- Work on your character's low points / conflict scenes

STABLE
- Doodle Happy Thoughts
- Read over your latest sketch or scene
- Freewrite 100 words (no editing)

WIP
- Doodle or brainstorm ideas
- Affirm "I am a work in progress"
- Freewrite 500 words or rework a scene

HAPPY
- Doodle your character's happy place
- Write for 60 minutes (split into 20-min sessions with breaks)
- Optional: Edit or expand on scenes

JOYFUL
- Doodle your personal happy place or story idea
- Write for 60–90 minutes (multiple sessions)
- Optional: start a second writing session
- Reflect or plan next steps

Write Draw Journal Craft Here

Writing Goals

Week: _____

Mood/Emotion Tracker

○ ○ ○ ○ ○
SAD STABLE WIP HAPPY JOYFUL
         ⟷

Doodle Space:

Writing Goals for Your Project

Writing Goals for The Week:

What I'm Proud of This Week:

Emotional Writing Suggestions

SAD
- Doodle or sketch something comforting
- Write down one small thing that went well today
- Work on your character's low points / conflict scenes

STABLE
- Doodle Happy Thoughts
- Read over your latest sketch or scene
- Freewrite 100 words (no editing)

WIP
- Doodle or brainstorm ideas
- Affirm "I am a work in progress"
- Freewrite 500 words or rework a scene

HAPPY
- Doodle your character's happy place
- Write for 60 minutes (split into 20-min sessions with breaks)
- Optional: Edit or expand on scenes

JOYFUL
- Doodle your personal happy place or story idea
- Write for 60–90 minutes (multiple sessions)
- Optional: start a second writing session
- Reflect or plan next steps

Write Draw Journal Craft Here

Writing Goals

Week: _____

Mood/Emotion Tracker

○ ○ ○ ○ ○
SAD STABLE WIP HAPPY JOYFUL
         ↔

Doodle Space:

Writing Goals for Your Project

Writing Goals for The Week:

What I'm Proud of This Week:

Emotional Writing Suggestions

SAD
- Doodle or sketch something comforting
- Write down one small thing that went well today
- Work on your character's low points / conflict scenes

STABLE
- Doodle Happy Thoughts
- Read over your latest sketch or scene
- Freewrite 100 words (no editing)

WIP
- Doodle or brainstorm ideas
- Affirm "I am a work in progress"
- Freewrite 500 words or rework a scene

HAPPY
- Doodle your character's happy place
- Write for 60 minutes (split into 20-min sessions with breaks)
- Optional: Edit or expand on scenes

JOYFUL
- Doodle your personal happy place or story idea
- Write for 60–90 minutes (multiple sessions)
- Optional: start a second writing session
- Reflect or plan next steps

Write Draw Journal Craft Here

Writing Goals

Week: _____

Mood/Emotion Tracker

○ ○ ○ ○ ○
SAD STABLE WIP ⟷ HAPPY JOYFUL

Doodle Space:

Writing Goals for Your Project

Writing Goals for The Week:

What I'm Proud of This Week:

Emotional Writing Suggestions

SAD
- Doodle or sketch something comforting
- Write down one small thing that went well today
- Work on your character's low points / conflict scenes

STABLE
- Doodle Happy Thoughts
- Read over your latest sketch or scene
- Freewrite 100 words (no editing)

WIP
- Doodle or brainstorm ideas
- Affirm "I am a work in progress"
- Freewrite 500 words or rework a scene

HAPPY
- Doodle your character's happy place
- Write for 60 minutes (split into 20-min sessions with breaks)
- Optional: Edit or expand on scenes

JOYFUL
- Doodle your personal happy place or story idea
- Write for 60–90 minutes (multiple sessions)
- Optional: start a second writing session
- Reflect or plan next steps

Write Draw Journal Craft Here

Writing Goals

Week: _____

Mood/Emotion Tracker

○ ○ ○ ○ ○
SAD STABLE WIP HAPPY JOYFUL
        ↔

Doodle Space:

Writing Goals for Your Project

Writing Goals for The Week:

What I'm Proud of This Week:

Emotional Writing Suggestions

SAD
- Doodle or sketch something comforting
- Write down one small thing that went well today
- Work on your character's low points / conflict scenes

STABLE
- Doodle Happy Thoughts
- Read over your latest sketch or scene
- Freewrite 100 words (no editing)

WIP
- Doodle or brainstorm ideas
- Affirm "I am a work in progress"
- Freewrite 500 words or rework a scene

HAPPY
- Doodle your character's happy place
- Write for 60 minutes (split into 20-min sessions with breaks)
- Optional: Edit or expand on scenes

JOYFUL
- Doodle your personal happy place or story idea
- Write for 60–90 minutes (multiple sessions)
- Optional: start a second writing session
- Reflect or plan next steps

Write Draw Journal Craft Here

Writing Goals

Week: _____

Mood/Emotion Tracker

○ ○ ○ ○ ○
SAD STABLE WIP HAPPY JOYFUL
              ↔

Doodle Space:

Writing Goals for Your Project

Writing Goals for The Week:

What I'm Proud of This Week:

Emotional Writing Suggestions

SAD
- Doodle or sketch something comforting
- Write down one small thing that went well today
- Work on your character's low points / conflict scenes

STABLE
- Doodle Happy Thoughts
- Read over your latest sketch or scene
- Freewrite 100 words (no editing)

WIP
- Doodle or brainstorm ideas
- Affirm "I am a work in progress"
- Freewrite 500 words or rework a scene

HAPPY
- Doodle your character's happy place
- Write for 60 minutes (split into 20-min sessions with breaks)
- Optional: Edit or expand on scenes

JOYFUL
- Doodle your personal happy place or story idea
- Write for 60–90 minutes (multiple sessions)
- Optional: start a second writing session
- Reflect or plan next steps

Write Draw Journal Craft Here

Writing Goals

Week: _____

Mood/Emotion Tracker

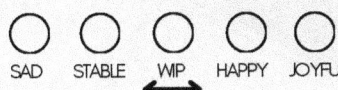

SAD   STABLE   WIP   HAPPY   JOYFUL

Doodle Space:

Writing Goals for Your Project

Writing Goals for The Week:

What I'm Proud of This Week:

Emotional Writing Suggestions

SAD
- Doodle or sketch something comforting
- Write down one small thing that went well today
- Work on your character's low points / conflict scenes

STABLE
- Doodle Happy Thoughts
- Read over your latest sketch or scene
- Freewrite 100 words (no editing)

WIP
- Doodle or brainstorm ideas
- Affirm "I am a work in progress"
- Freewrite 500 words or rework a scene

HAPPY
- Doodle your character's happy place
- Write for 60 minutes (split into 20-min sessions with breaks)
- Optional: Edit or expand on scenes

JOYFUL
- Doodle your personal happy place or story idea
- Write for 60–90 minutes (multiple sessions)
- Optional: start a second writing session
- Reflect or plan next steps

Write Draw Journal Craft Here

Writing Goals

Week: _____

Mood/Emotion Tracker

○ ○ ○ ○ ○
SAD STABLE WIP HAPPY JOYFUL
            ↔

Doodle Space:

Writing Goals for Your Project

Writing Goals for The Week:

What I'm Proud of This Week:

Emotional Writing Suggestions

SAD
- Doodle or sketch something comforting
- Write down one small thing that went well today
- Work on your character's low points / conflict scenes

STABLE
- Doodle Happy Thoughts
- Read over your latest sketch or scene
- Freewrite 100 words (no editing)

WIP
- Doodle or brainstorm ideas
- Affirm "I am a work in progress"
- Freewrite 500 words or rework a scene

HAPPY
- Doodle your character's happy place
- Write for 60 minutes (split into 20-min sessions with breaks)
- Optional: Edit or expand on scenes

JOYFUL
- Doodle your personal happy place or story idea
- Write for 60–90 minutes (multiple sessions)
- Optional: start a second writing session
- Reflect or plan next steps

Write Draw Journal Craft Here

Writing Goals

Week: _____

Mood/Emotion Tracker

○ ○ ○ ○ ○
SAD STABLE WIP HAPPY JOYFUL
↔

Doodle Space:

Writing Goals for Your Project

Writing Goals for The Week:

What I'm Proud of This Week:

Emotional Writing Suggestions

SAD
- Doodle or sketch something comforting
- Write down one small thing that went well today
- Work on your character's low points / conflict scenes

STABLE
- Doodle Happy Thoughts
- Read over your latest sketch or scene
- Freewrite 100 words (no editing)

WIP
- Doodle or brainstorm ideas
- Affirm "I am a work in progress"
- Freewrite 500 words or rework a scene

HAPPY
- Doodle your character's happy place
- Write for 60 minutes (split into 20-min sessions with breaks)
- Optional: Edit or expand on scenes

JOYFUL
- Doodle your personal happy place or story idea
- Write for 60–90 minutes (multiple sessions)
- Optional: start a second writing session
- Reflect or plan next steps

Write Draw Journal Craft Here

Writing Goals

Week: _____

Mood/Emotion Tracker

○ ○ ○ ○ ○
SAD STABLE WIP HAPPY JOYFUL
⟷

Doodle Space:

Writing Goals for Your Project

Writing Goals for The Week:

What I'm Proud of This Week:

Emotional Writing Suggestions

SAD
- Doodle or sketch something comforting
- Write down one small thing that went well today
- Work on your character's low points / conflict scenes

STABLE
- Doodle Happy Thoughts
- Read over your latest sketch or scene
- Freewrite 100 words (no editing)

WIP
- Doodle or brainstorm ideas
- Affirm "I am a work in progress"
- Freewrite 500 words or rework a scene

HAPPY
- Doodle your character's happy place
- Write for 60 minutes (split into 20-min sessions with breaks)
- Optional: Edit or expand on scenes

JOYFUL
- Doodle your personal happy place or story idea
- Write for 60–90 minutes (multiple sessions)
- Optional: start a second writing session
- Reflect or plan next steps

Write Draw Journal Craft Here

Writing Goals

Week: _____

Mood/Emotion Tracker

○ ○ ○ ○ ○
SAD STABLE WIP HAPPY JOYFUL
↔

Doodle Space:

Writing Goals for Your Project

Writing Goals for The Week:

What I'm Proud of This Week:

Emotional Writing Suggestions

SAD
- Doodle or sketch something comforting
- Write down one small thing that went well today
- Work on your character's low points / conflict scenes

STABLE
- Doodle Happy Thoughts
- Read over your latest sketch or scene
- Freewrite 100 words (no editing)

WIP
- Doodle or brainstorm ideas
- Affirm "I am a work in progress"
- Freewrite 500 words or rework a scene

HAPPY
- Doodle your character's happy place
- Write for 60 minutes (split into 20-min sessions with breaks)
- Optional: Edit or expand on scenes

JOYFUL
- Doodle your personal happy place or story idea
- Write for 60–90 minutes (multiple sessions)
- Optional: start a second writing session
- Reflect or plan next steps

Write Draw Journal Craft Here

Writing Goals

Week: _____

Mood/Emotion Tracker

○ ○ ○ ○ ○
SAD STABLE WIP HAPPY JOYFUL
         ↔

Doodle Space:

Writing Goals for Your Project

Writing Goals for The Week:

What I'm Proud of This Week:

Emotional Writing Suggestions

SAD
- Doodle or sketch something comforting
- Write down one small thing that went well today
- Work on your character's low points / conflict scenes

STABLE
- Doodle Happy Thoughts
- Read over your latest sketch or scene
- Freewrite 100 words (no editing)

WIP
- Doodle or brainstorm ideas
- Affirm "I am a work in progress"
- Freewrite 500 words or rework a scene

HAPPY
- Doodle your character's happy place
- Write for 60 minutes (split into 20-min sessions with breaks)
- Optional: Edit or expand on scenes

JOYFUL
- Doodle your personal happy place or story idea
- Write for 60–90 minutes (multiple sessions)
- Optional: start a second writing session
- Reflect or plan next steps

Write Draw Journal Craft Here

Writing Goals

Week: _____

Mood/Emotion Tracker

○ ○ ○ ○ ○
SAD STABLE WIP HAPPY JOYFUL
         ↔

Doodle Space:

Writing Goals for Your Project

Writing Goals for The Week:

What I'm Proud of This Week:

Emotional Writing Suggestions

SAD
- Doodle or sketch something comforting
- Write down one small thing that went well today
- Work on your character's low points / conflict scenes

STABLE
- Doodle Happy Thoughts
- Read over your latest sketch or scene
- Freewrite 100 words (no editing)

WIP
- Doodle or brainstorm ideas
- Affirm "I am a work in progress"
- Freewrite 500 words or rework a scene

HAPPY
- Doodle your character's happy place
- Write for 60 minutes (split into 20-min sessions with breaks)
- Optional: Edit or expand on scenes

JOYFUL
- Doodle your personal happy place or story idea
- Write for 60–90 minutes (multiple sessions)
- Optional: start a second writing session
- Reflect or plan next steps

Write Draw Journal Craft Here

Writing Goals

Week: _____

Mood/Emotion Tracker

○ ○ ○ ○ ○
SAD STABLE WIP HAPPY JOYFUL
         ↔

Doodle Space:

Writing Goals for Your Project

Writing Goals for The Week:

What I'm Proud of This Week:

Emotional Writing Suggestions

SAD
- Doodle or sketch something comforting
- Write down one small thing that went well today
- Work on your character's low points / conflict scenes

STABLE
- Doodle Happy Thoughts
- Read over your latest sketch or scene
- Freewrite 100 words (no editing)

WIP
- Doodle or brainstorm ideas
- Affirm "I am a work in progress"
- Freewrite 500 words or rework a scene

HAPPY
- Doodle your character's happy place
- Write for 60 minutes (split into 20-min sessions with breaks)
- Optional: Edit or expand on scenes

JOYFUL
- Doodle your personal happy place or story idea
- Write for 60–90 minutes (multiple sessions)
- Optional: start a second writing session
- Reflect or plan next steps

Write Draw Journal Craft Here

Writing Goals

Week: _____

Mood/Emotion Tracker

○ ○ ○ ○ ○
SAD STABLE WIP HAPPY JOYFUL
         ←→

Doodle Space:

Writing Goals for Your Project

Writing Goals for The Week:

What I'm Proud of This Week:

Emotional Writing Suggestions

SAD
- Doodle or sketch something comforting
- Write down one small thing that went well today
- Work on your character's low points / conflict scenes

STABLE
- Doodle Happy Thoughts
- Read over your latest sketch or scene
- Freewrite 100 words (no editing)

WIP
- Doodle or brainstorm ideas
- Affirm "I am a work in progress"
- Freewrite 500 words or rework a scene

HAPPY
- Doodle your character's happy place
- Write for 60 minutes (split into 20-min sessions with breaks)
- Optional: Edit or expand on scenes

JOYFUL
- Doodle your personal happy place or story idea
- Write for 60–90 minutes (multiple sessions)
- Optional: start a second writing session
- Reflect or plan next steps

Write Draw Journal Craft Here

Writing Goals

Week: _____

Mood/Emotion Tracker

○ ○ ○ ○ ○
SAD STABLE WIP HAPPY JOYFUL
           ↔

Doodle Space:

Writing Goals for Your Project

Writing Goals for The Week:

What I'm Proud of This Week:

Emotional Writing Suggestions

SAD
- Doodle or sketch something comforting
- Write down one small thing that went well today
- Work on your character's low points / conflict scenes

STABLE
- Doodle Happy Thoughts
- Read over your latest sketch or scene
- Freewrite 100 words (no editing)

WIP
- Doodle or brainstorm ideas
- Affirm "I am a work in progress"
- Freewrite 500 words or rework a scene

HAPPY
- Doodle your character's happy place
- Write for 60 minutes (split into 20-min sessions with breaks)
- Optional: Edit or expand on scenes

JOYFUL
- Doodle your personal happy place or story idea
- Write for 60–90 minutes (multiple sessions)
- Optional: start a second writing session
- Reflect or plan next steps

Write Draw Journal Craft Here

Writing Goals

Week: _____

Mood/Emotion Tracker

○ ○ ○ ○ ○
SAD STABLE WIP HAPPY JOYFUL
       ←→

Doodle Space:

Writing Goals for Your Project

Writing Goals for The Week:

What I'm Proud of This Week:

Emotional Writing Suggestions

SAD
- Doodle or sketch something comforting
- Write down one small thing that went well today
- Work on your character's low points / conflict scenes

STABLE
- Doodle Happy Thoughts
- Read over your latest sketch or scene
- Freewrite 100 words (no editing)

WIP
- Doodle or brainstorm ideas
- Affirm "I am a work in progress"
- Freewrite 500 words or rework a scene

HAPPY
- Doodle your character's happy place
- Write for 60 minutes (split into 20-min sessions with breaks)
- Optional: Edit or expand on scenes

JOYFUL
- Doodle your personal happy place or story idea
- Write for 60–90 minutes (multiple sessions)
- Optional: start a second writing session
- Reflect or plan next steps

Write Draw Journal Craft Here

Writing Goals

Week: _____

Mood/Emotion Tracker

○ ○ ○ ○ ○
SAD STABLE WIP HAPPY JOYFUL
          ↔

Doodle Space:

Writing Goals for Your Project

Writing Goals for The Week:

What I'm Proud of This Week:

Emotional Writing Suggestions

SAD
- Doodle or sketch something comforting
- Write down one small thing that went well today
- Work on your character's low points / conflict scenes

STABLE
- Doodle Happy Thoughts
- Read over your latest sketch or scene
- Freewrite 100 words (no editing)

WIP
- Doodle or brainstorm ideas
- Affirm "I am a work in progress"
- Freewrite 500 words or rework a scene

HAPPY
- Doodle your character's happy place
- Write for 60 minutes (split into 20-min sessions with breaks)
- Optional: Edit or expand on scenes

JOYFUL
- Doodle your personal happy place or story idea
- Write for 60–90 minutes (multiple sessions)
- Optional: start a second writing session
- Reflect or plan next steps

Write Draw Journal Craft Here

Writing Goals

Week: _____

Mood/Emotion Tracker

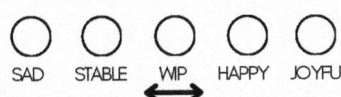

Doodle Space:

Writing Goals for Your Project

Writing Goals for The Week:

What I'm Proud of This Week:

Emotional Writing Suggestions

SAD
- Doodle or sketch something comforting
- Write down one small thing that went well today
- Work on your character's low points / conflict scenes

STABLE
- Doodle Happy Thoughts
- Read over your latest sketch or scene
- Freewrite 100 words (no editing)

WIP
- Doodle or brainstorm ideas
- Affirm "I am a work in progress"
- Freewrite 500 words or rework a scene

HAPPY
- Doodle your character's happy place
- Write for 60 minutes (split into 20-min sessions with breaks)
- Optional: Edit or expand on scenes

JOYFUL
- Doodle your personal happy place or story idea
- Write for 60–90 minutes (multiple sessions)
- Optional: start a second writing session
- Reflect or plan next steps

Write Draw Journal Craft Here

Writing Goals

Week: _____

Mood/Emotion Tracker

○ ○ ○ ○ ○
SAD STABLE WIP HAPPY JOYFUL
         ↔

Doodle Space:

Writing Goals for Your Project

Writing Goals for The Week:

Emotional Writing Suggestions

SAD
- Doodle or sketch something comforting
- Write down one small thing that went well today
- Work on your character's low points / conflict scenes

STABLE
- Doodle Happy Thoughts
- Read over your latest sketch or scene
- Freewrite 100 words (no editing)

WIP
- Doodle or brainstorm ideas
- Affirm "I am a work in progress"
- Freewrite 500 words or rework a scene

HAPPY
- Doodle your character's happy place
- Write for 60 minutes (split into 20-min sessions with breaks)
- Optional: Edit or expand on scenes

JOYFUL
- Doodle your personal happy place or story idea
- Write for 60–90 minutes (multiple sessions)
- Optional: start a second writing session
- Reflect or plan next steps

What I'm Proud of This Week:

Write Draw Journal Craft Here

Writing Goals

Week: _____

Mood/Emotion Tracker

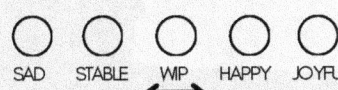

○ ○ ○ ○ ○
SAD STABLE WIP HAPPY JOYFUL

Emotional Writing Suggestions

SAD
- Doodle or sketch something comforting
- Write down one small thing that went well today
- Work on your character's low points / conflict scenes

STABLE
- Doodle Happy Thoughts
- Read over your latest sketch or scene
- Freewrite 100 words (no editing)

WIP
- Doodle or brainstorm ideas
- Affirm "I am a work in progress"
- Freewrite 500 words or rework a scene

HAPPY
- Doodle your character's happy place
- Write for 60 minutes (split into 20-min sessions with breaks)
- Optional: Edit or expand on scenes

JOYFUL
- Doodle your personal happy place or story idea
- Write for 60–90 minutes (multiple sessions)
- Optional: start a second writing session
- Reflect or plan next steps

Doodle Space:

Writing Goals for Your Project

Writing Goals for The Week:

What I'm Proud of This Week:

Write Draw Journal Craft Here

Writing Goals

Week: _____

Mood/Emotion Tracker

○ ○ ○ ○ ○
SAD STABLE WIP HAPPY JOYFUL
⟷

Doodle Space:

Writing Goals for Your Project

Writing Goals for The Week:

What I'm Proud of This Week:

Emotional Writing Suggestions

SAD
- Doodle or sketch something comforting
- Write down one small thing that went well today
- Work on your character's low points / conflict scenes

STABLE
- Doodle Happy Thoughts
- Read over your latest sketch or scene
- Freewrite 100 words (no editing)

WIP
- Doodle or brainstorm ideas
- Affirm "I am a work in progress"
- Freewrite 500 words or rework a scene

HAPPY
- Doodle your character's happy place
- Write for 60 minutes (split into 20-min sessions with breaks)
- Optional: Edit or expand on scenes

JOYFUL
- Doodle your personal happy place or story idea
- Write for 60–90 minutes (multiple sessions)
- Optional: start a second writing session
- Reflect or plan next steps

Write Draw Journal Craft Here

Writing Goals

Week: _____

Mood/Emotion Tracker

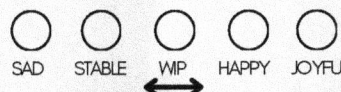

SAD STABLE WIP HAPPY JOYFUL

Doodle Space:

Writing Goals for Your Project

Writing Goals for The Week:

What I'm Proud of This Week:

Emotional Writing Suggestions

SAD
- Doodle or sketch something comforting
- Write down one small thing that went well today
- Work on your character's low points / conflict scenes

STABLE
- Doodle Happy Thoughts
- Read over your latest sketch or scene
- Freewrite 100 words (no editing)

WIP
- Doodle or brainstorm ideas
- Affirm "I am a work in progress"
- Freewrite 500 words or rework a scene

HAPPY
- Doodle your character's happy place
- Write for 60 minutes (split into 20-min sessions with breaks)
- Optional: Edit or expand on scenes

JOYFUL
- Doodle your personal happy place or story idea
- Write for 60–90 minutes (multiple sessions)
- Optional: start a second writing session
- Reflect or plan next steps

Write Draw Journal Craft Here

Writing Goals

Week: _____

Mood/Emotion Tracker

○ ○ ○ ○ ○
SAD STABLE WIP ↔ HAPPY JOYFUL

Doodle Space:

Writing Goals for Your Project

Writing Goals for The Week:

What I'm Proud of This Week:

Emotional Writing Suggestions

SAD
- Doodle or sketch something comforting
- Write down one small thing that went well today
- Work on your character's low points / conflict scenes

STABLE
- Doodle Happy Thoughts
- Read over your latest sketch or scene
- Freewrite 100 words (no editing)

WIP
- Doodle or brainstorm ideas
- Affirm "I am a work in progress"
- Freewrite 500 words or rework a scene

HAPPY
- Doodle your character's happy place
- Write for 60 minutes (split into 20-min sessions with breaks)
- Optional: Edit or expand on scenes

JOYFUL
- Doodle your personal happy place or story idea
- Write for 60–90 minutes (multiple sessions)
- Optional: start a second writing session
- Reflect or plan next steps

Write Draw Journal Craft Here

Writing Goals

Week: _____

Mood/Emotion Tracker

○ ○ ○ ○ ○
SAD STABLE WIP HAPPY JOYFUL
         ←→

Doodle Space:

Writing Goals for Your Project

Writing Goals for The Week:

What I'm Proud of This Week:

Emotional Writing Suggestions

SAD
- Doodle or sketch something comforting
- Write down one small thing that went well today
- Work on your character's low points / conflict scenes

STABLE
- Doodle Happy Thoughts
- Read over your latest sketch or scene
- Freewrite 100 words (no editing)

WIP
- Doodle or brainstorm ideas
- Affirm "I am a work in progress"
- Freewrite 500 words or rework a scene

HAPPY
- Doodle your character's happy place
- Write for 60 minutes (split into 20-min sessions with breaks)
- Optional: Edit or expand on scenes

JOYFUL
- Doodle your personal happy place or story idea
- Write for 60–90 minutes (multiple sessions)
- Optional: start a second writing session
- Reflect or plan next steps

Write Draw Journal Craft Here

Writing Goals

Week: _____

Mood/Emotion Tracker

○ ○ ○ ○ ○
SAD STABLE WIP HAPPY JOYFUL
         ⟷

Doodle Space:

Writing Goals for Your Project

Writing Goals for The Week:

What I'm Proud of This Week:

Emotional Writing Suggestions

SAD
- Doodle or sketch something comforting
- Write down one small thing that went well today
- Work on your character's low points / conflict scenes

STABLE
- Doodle Happy Thoughts
- Read over your latest sketch or scene
- Freewrite 100 words (no editing)

WIP
- Doodle or brainstorm ideas
- Affirm "I am a work in progress"
- Freewrite 500 words or rework a scene

HAPPY
- Doodle your character's happy place
- Write for 60 minutes (split into 20-min sessions with breaks)
- Optional: Edit or expand on scenes

JOYFUL
- Doodle your personal happy place or story idea
- Write for 60–90 minutes (multiple sessions)
- Optional: start a second writing session
- Reflect or plan next steps

Write Draw Journal Craft Here

Writing Goals

Week: _____

Mood/Emotion Tracker

○ ○ ○ ○ ○
SAD STABLE WIP HAPPY JOYFUL
          ←→

Doodle Space:

Writing Goals for Your Project

Writing Goals for The Week:

What I'm Proud of This Week:

Emotional Writing Suggestions

SAD
- Doodle or sketch something comforting
- Write down one small thing that went well today
- Work on your character's low points / conflict scenes

STABLE
- Doodle Happy Thoughts
- Read over your latest sketch or scene
- Freewrite 100 words (no editing)

WIP
- Doodle or brainstorm ideas
- Affirm "I am a work in progress"
- Freewrite 500 words or rework a scene

HAPPY
- Doodle your character's happy place
- Write for 60 minutes (split into 20-min sessions with breaks)
- Optional: Edit or expand on scenes

JOYFUL
- Doodle your personal happy place or story idea
- Write for 60–90 minutes (multiple sessions)
- Optional: start a second writing session
- Reflect or plan next steps

Write Draw Journal Craft Here

Writing Goals

Week: _____

Mood/Emotion Tracker

○ ○ ○ ○ ○
SAD STABLE WIP HAPPY JOYFUL
⟷

Doodle Space:

Writing Goals for Your Project

Writing Goals for The Week:

Emotional Writing Suggestions

SAD
- Doodle or sketch something comforting
- Write down one small thing that went well today
- Work on your character's low points / conflict scenes

STABLE
- Doodle Happy Thoughts
- Read over your latest sketch or scene
- Freewrite 100 words (no editing)

WIP
- Doodle or brainstorm ideas
- Affirm "I am a work in progress"
- Freewrite 500 words or rework a scene

HAPPY
- Doodle your character's happy place
- Write for 60 minutes (split into 20-min sessions with breaks)
- Optional: Edit or expand on scenes

JOYFUL
- Doodle your personal happy place or story idea
- Write for 60–90 minutes (multiple sessions)
- Optional: start a second writing session
- Reflect or plan next steps

What I'm Proud of This Week:

Write Draw Journal Craft Here

Writing Goals

Week: _____

Mood/Emotion Tracker

○ ○ ○ ○ ○
SAD STABLE WIP HAPPY JOYFUL
         ←→

Doodle Space:

Writing Goals for Your Project

Writing Goals for The Week:

What I'm Proud of This Week:

Emotional Writing Suggestions

SAD
- Doodle or sketch something comforting
- Write down one small thing that went well today
- Work on your character's low points / conflict scenes

STABLE
- Doodle Happy Thoughts
- Read over your latest sketch or scene
- Freewrite 100 words (no editing)

WIP
- Doodle or brainstorm ideas
- Affirm "I am a work in progress"
- Freewrite 500 words or rework a scene

HAPPY
- Doodle your character's happy place
- Write for 60 minutes (split into 20-min sessions with breaks)
- Optional: Edit or expand on scenes

JOYFUL
- Doodle your personal happy place or story idea
- Write for 60–90 minutes (multiple sessions)
- Optional: start a second writing session
- Reflect or plan next steps

Write Draw Journal Craft Here

Writing Goals

Week: _____

Mood/Emotion Tracker

○ ○ ○ ○ ○
SAD STABLE WIP HAPPY JOYFUL
         ↔

Doodle Space:

Writing Goals for Your Project

Writing Goals for The Week:

What I'm Proud of This Week:

Emotional Writing Suggestions

SAD
- Doodle or sketch something comforting
- Write down one small thing that went well today
- Work on your character's low points / conflict scenes

STABLE
- Doodle Happy Thoughts
- Read over your latest sketch or scene
- Freewrite 100 words (no editing)

WIP
- Doodle or brainstorm ideas
- Affirm "I am a work in progress"
- Freewrite 500 words or rework a scene

HAPPY
- Doodle your character's happy place
- Write for 60 minutes (split into 20-min sessions with breaks)
- Optional: Edit or expand on scenes

JOYFUL
- Doodle your personal happy place or story idea
- Write for 60–90 minutes (multiple sessions)
- Optional: start a second writing session
- Reflect or plan next steps

Write Draw Journal Craft Here

Writing Goals

Week: _____

Mood/Emotion Tracker

○ ○ ○ ○ ○
SAD STABLE WIP HAPPY JOYFUL
         ↔

Doodle Space:

Writing Goals for Your Project

Writing Goals for The Week:

Emotional Writing Suggestions

SAD
- Doodle or sketch something comforting
- Write down one small thing that went well today
- Work on your character's low points / conflict scenes

STABLE
- Doodle Happy Thoughts
- Read over your latest sketch or scene
- Freewrite 100 words (no editing)

WIP
- Doodle or brainstorm ideas
- Affirm "I am a work in progress"
- Freewrite 500 words or rework a scene

HAPPY
- Doodle your character's happy place
- Write for 60 minutes (split into 20-min sessions with breaks)
- Optional: Edit or expand on scenes

JOYFUL
- Doodle your personal happy place or story idea
- Write for 60–90 minutes (multiple sessions)
- Optional: start a second writing session
- Reflect or plan next steps

What I'm Proud of This Week:

Write Draw Journal Craft Here

Writing Goals

Week: _____

Mood/Emotion Tracker

◯ ◯ ◯ ◯ ◯
SAD STABLE WIP HAPPY JOYFUL
         ⟷

Doodle Space:

Writing Goals for Your Project

Writing Goals for The Week:

What I'm Proud of This Week:

Emotional Writing Suggestions

SAD
- Doodle or sketch something comforting
- Write down one small thing that went well today
- Work on your character's low points / conflict scenes

STABLE
- Doodle Happy Thoughts
- Read over your latest sketch or scene
- Freewrite 100 words (no editing)

WIP
- Doodle or brainstorm ideas
- Affirm "I am a work in progress"
- Freewrite 500 words or rework a scene

HAPPY
- Doodle your character's happy place
- Write for 60 minutes (split into 20-min sessions with breaks)
- Optional: Edit or expand on scenes

JOYFUL
- Doodle your personal happy place or story idea
- Write for 60–90 minutes (multiple sessions)
- Optional: start a second writing session
- Reflect or plan next steps

Write Draw Journal Craft Here

Writing Goals

Week: _____

Mood/Emotion Tracker

○ ○ ○ ○ ○
SAD STABLE WIP HAPPY JOYFUL
         ↔

Doodle Space:

Writing Goals for Your Project

Writing Goals for The Week:

What I'm Proud of This Week:

Emotional Writing Suggestions

SAD
- Doodle or sketch something comforting
- Write down one small thing that went well today
- Work on your character's low points / conflict scenes

STABLE
- Doodle Happy Thoughts
- Read over your latest sketch or scene
- Freewrite 100 words (no editing)

WIP
- Doodle or brainstorm ideas
- Affirm "I am a work in progress"
- Freewrite 500 words or rework a scene

HAPPY
- Doodle your character's happy place
- Write for 60 minutes (split into 20-min sessions with breaks)
- Optional: Edit or expand on scenes

JOYFUL
- Doodle your personal happy place or story idea
- Write for 60–90 minutes (multiple sessions)
- Optional: start a second writing session
- Reflect or plan next steps

Write Draw Journal Craft Here

Writing Goals

Week: _____

Mood/Emotion Tracker

○ ○ ○ ○ ○
SAD STABLE WIP HAPPY JOYFUL
        ⟷

Doodle Space:

Writing Goals for Your Project

Writing Goals for The Week:

What I'm Proud of This Week:

Emotional Writing Suggestions

SAD
- Doodle or sketch something comforting
- Write down one small thing that went well today
- Work on your character's low points / conflict scenes

STABLE
- Doodle Happy Thoughts
- Read over your latest sketch or scene
- Freewrite 100 words (no editing)

WIP
- Doodle or brainstorm ideas
- Affirm "I am a work in progress"
- Freewrite 500 words or rework a scene

HAPPY
- Doodle your character's happy place
- Write for 60 minutes (split into 20-min sessions with breaks)
- Optional: Edit or expand on scenes

JOYFUL
- Doodle your personal happy place or story idea
- Write for 60–90 minutes (multiple sessions)
- Optional: start a second writing session
- Reflect or plan next steps

Write Draw Journal Craft Here

Writing Goals

Week: _____

Mood/Emotion Tracker

○ ○ ○ ○ ○
SAD STABLE WIP HAPPY JOYFUL
      ↔

Doodle Space:

Writing Goals for Your Project

Writing Goals for The Week:

What I'm Proud of This Week:

Emotional Writing Suggestions

SAD
- Doodle or sketch something comforting
- Write down one small thing that went well today
- Work on your character's low points / conflict scenes

STABLE
- Doodle Happy Thoughts
- Read over your latest sketch or scene
- Freewrite 100 words (no editing)

WIP
- Doodle or brainstorm ideas
- Affirm "I am a work in progress"
- Freewrite 500 words or rework a scene

HAPPY
- Doodle your character's happy place
- Write for 60 minutes (split into 20-min sessions with breaks)
- Optional: Edit or expand on scenes

JOYFUL
- Doodle your personal happy place or story idea
- Write for 60–90 minutes (multiple sessions)
- Optional: start a second writing session
- Reflect or plan next steps

Write Draw Journal Craft Here

Writing Goals

Week: _____

Mood/Emotion Tracker

○ ○ ○ ○ ○
SAD STABLE WIP HAPPY JOYFUL
　　　　↔

Doodle Space:

Writing Goals for Your Project

Writing Goals for The Week:

What I'm Proud of This Week:

Emotional Writing Suggestions

SAD
- Doodle or sketch something comforting
- Write down one small thing that went well today
- Work on your character's low points / conflict scenes

STABLE
- Doodle Happy Thoughts
- Read over your latest sketch or scene
- Freewrite 100 words (no editing)

WIP
- Doodle or brainstorm ideas
- Affirm "I am a work in progress"
- Freewrite 500 words or rework a scene

HAPPY
- Doodle your character's happy place
- Write for 60 minutes (split into 20-min sessions with breaks)
- Optional: Edit or expand on scenes

JOYFUL
- Doodle your personal happy place or story idea
- Write for 60–90 minutes (multiple sessions)
- Optional: start a second writing session
- Reflect or plan next steps

Write Draw Journal Craft Here

Writing Goals

Week: _____

Mood/Emotion Tracker

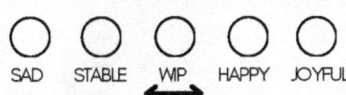

○ ○ ○ ○ ○
SAD STABLE WIP HAPPY JOYFUL
         ↔

Doodle Space:

Writing Goals for Your Project

Writing Goals for The Week:

What I'm Proud of This Week:

Emotional Writing Suggestions

SAD
- Doodle or sketch something comforting
- Write down one small thing that went well today
- Work on your character's low points / conflict scenes

STABLE
- Doodle Happy Thoughts
- Read over your latest sketch or scene
- Freewrite 100 words (no editing)

WIP
- Doodle or brainstorm ideas
- Affirm "I am a work in progress"
- Freewrite 500 words or rework a scene

HAPPY
- Doodle your character's happy place
- Write for 60 minutes (split into 20-min sessions with breaks)
- Optional: Edit or expand on scenes

JOYFUL
- Doodle your personal happy place or story idea
- Write for 60–90 minutes (multiple sessions)
- Optional: start a second writing session
- Reflect or plan next steps

Write Draw Journal Craft Here

Writing Goals

Week: _____

Mood/Emotion Tracker

○ ○ ○ ○ ○
SAD STABLE WIP HAPPY JOYFUL
           ↔

Doodle Space:

Writing Goals for Your Project

Writing Goals for The Week:

What I'm Proud of This Week:

Emotional Writing Suggestions

SAD
- Doodle or sketch something comforting
- Write down one small thing that went well today
- Work on your character's low points / conflict scenes

STABLE
- Doodle Happy Thoughts
- Read over your latest sketch or scene
- Freewrite 100 words (no editing)

WIP
- Doodle or brainstorm ideas
- Affirm "I am a work in progress"
- Freewrite 500 words or rework a scene

HAPPY
- Doodle your character's happy place
- Write for 60 minutes (split into 20-min sessions with breaks)
- Optional: Edit or expand on scenes

JOYFUL
- Doodle your personal happy place or story idea
- Write for 60–90 minutes (multiple sessions)
- Optional: start a second writing session
- Reflect or plan next steps

Write Draw Journal Craft Here

Writing Goals

Week: _____

Mood/Emotion Tracker

○ ○ ○ ○ ○
SAD STABLE WIP HAPPY JOYFUL
        ⟷

Doodle Space:

Writing Goals for Your Project

Writing Goals for The Week:

What I'm Proud of This Week:

Emotional Writing Suggestions

SAD
- Doodle or sketch something comforting
- Write down one small thing that went well today
- Work on your character's low points / conflict scenes

STABLE
- Doodle Happy Thoughts
- Read over your latest sketch or scene
- Freewrite 100 words (no editing)

WIP
- Doodle or brainstorm ideas
- Affirm "I am a work in progress"
- Freewrite 500 words or rework a scene

HAPPY
- Doodle your character's happy place
- Write for 60 minutes (split into 20-min sessions with breaks)
- Optional: Edit or expand on scenes

JOYFUL
- Doodle your personal happy place or story idea
- Write for 60–90 minutes (multiple sessions)
- Optional: start a second writing session
- Reflect or plan next steps

Write Draw Journal Craft Here

Writing Goals

Week: _____

Mood/Emotion Tracker

○ ○ ○ ○ ○
SAD STABLE WIP HAPPY JOYFUL
         ↔

Doodle Space:

Writing Goals for Your Project

Writing Goals for The Week:

What I'm Proud of This Week:

Emotional Writing Suggestions

SAD
- Doodle or sketch something comforting
- Write down one small thing that went well today
- Work on your character's low points / conflict scenes

STABLE
- Doodle Happy Thoughts
- Read over your latest sketch or scene
- Freewrite 100 words (no editing)

WIP
- Doodle or brainstorm ideas
- Affirm "I am a work in progress"
- Freewrite 500 words or rework a scene

HAPPY
- Doodle your character's happy place
- Write for 60 minutes (split into 20-min sessions with breaks)
- Optional: Edit or expand on scenes

JOYFUL
- Doodle your personal happy place or story idea
- Write for 60–90 minutes (multiple sessions)
- Optional: start a second writing session
- Reflect or plan next steps

Write Draw Journal Craft Here

Writing Goals

Week: _____

Mood/Emotion Tracker

○ ○ ○ ○ ○
SAD STABLE WIP HAPPY JOYFUL
        ↔

Doodle Space:

Writing Goals for Your Project

Writing Goals for The Week:

What I'm Proud of This Week:

Emotional Writing Suggestions

SAD
- Doodle or sketch something comforting
- Write down one small thing that went well today
- Work on your character's low points / conflict scenes

STABLE
- Doodle Happy Thoughts
- Read over your latest sketch or scene
- Freewrite 100 words (no editing)

WIP
- Doodle or brainstorm ideas
- Affirm "I am a work in progress"
- Freewrite 500 words or rework a scene

HAPPY
- Doodle your character's happy place
- Write for 60 minutes (split into 20-min sessions with breaks)
- Optional: Edit or expand on scenes

JOYFUL
- Doodle your personal happy place or story idea
- Write for 60–90 minutes (multiple sessions)
- Optional: start a second writing session
- Reflect or plan next steps

Write Draw Journal Craft Here

Writing Goals

Week: _____

Mood/Emotion Tracker

○ ○ ○ ○ ○
SAD STABLE WIP HAPPY JOYFUL
         ⟷

Doodle Space:

Writing Goals for Your Project

Writing Goals for The Week:

What I'm Proud of This Week:

Emotional Writing Suggestions

SAD
- Doodle or sketch something comforting
- Write down one small thing that went well today
- Work on your character's low points / conflict scenes

STABLE
- Doodle Happy Thoughts
- Read over your latest sketch or scene
- Freewrite 100 words (no editing)

WIP
- Doodle or brainstorm ideas
- Affirm "I am a work in progress"
- Freewrite 500 words or rework a scene

HAPPY
- Doodle your character's happy place
- Write for 60 minutes (split into 20-min sessions with breaks)
- Optional: Edit or expand on scenes

JOYFUL
- Doodle your personal happy place or story idea
- Write for 60–90 minutes (multiple sessions)
- Optional: start a second writing session
- Reflect or plan next steps

Write Draw Journal Craft Here

Writing Goals

Week: _____

Mood/Emotion Tracker

○ ○ ○ ○ ○
SAD STABLE WIP HAPPY JOYFUL
         ↔

Doodle Space:

Writing Goals for Your Project

Writing Goals for The Week:

What I'm Proud of This Week:

Emotional Writing Suggestions

SAD
- Doodle or sketch something comforting
- Write down one small thing that went well today
- Work on your character's low points / conflict scenes

STABLE
- Doodle Happy Thoughts
- Read over your latest sketch or scene
- Freewrite 100 words (no editing)

WIP
- Doodle or brainstorm ideas
- Affirm "I am a work in progress"
- Freewrite 500 words or rework a scene

HAPPY
- Doodle your character's happy place
- Write for 60 minutes (split into 20-min sessions with breaks)
- Optional: Edit or expand on scenes

JOYFUL
- Doodle your personal happy place or story idea
- Write for 60–90 minutes (multiple sessions)
- Optional: start a second writing session
- Reflect or plan next steps

Write Draw Journal Craft Here

Writing Goals

Week: _____

Mood/Emotion Tracker

○ ○ ○ ○ ○
SAD STABLE WIP HAPPY JOYFUL
         ↔

Doodle Space:

Writing Goals for Your Project

Writing Goals for The Week:

What I'm Proud of This Week:

Emotional Writing Suggestions

SAD
- Doodle or sketch something comforting
- Write down one small thing that went well today
- Work on your character's low points / conflict scenes

STABLE
- Doodle Happy Thoughts
- Read over your latest sketch or scene
- Freewrite 100 words (no editing)

WIP
- Doodle or brainstorm ideas
- Affirm "I am a work in progress"
- Freewrite 500 words or rework a scene

HAPPY
- Doodle your character's happy place
- Write for 60 minutes (split into 20-min sessions with breaks)
- Optional: Edit or expand on scenes

JOYFUL
- Doodle your personal happy place or story idea
- Write for 60–90 minutes (multiple sessions)
- Optional: start a second writing session
- Reflect or plan next steps

Write Draw Journal Craft Here

Writing Goals

Week: _____

Mood/Emotion Tracker

○ ○ ○ ○ ○
SAD STABLE WIP HAPPY JOYFUL
⟵⟶

Doodle Space:

Writing Goals for Your Project

Writing Goals for The Week:

What I'm Proud of This Week:

Emotional Writing Suggestions

SAD
- Doodle or sketch something comforting
- Write down one small thing that went well today
- Work on your character's low points / conflict scenes

STABLE
- Doodle Happy Thoughts
- Read over your latest sketch or scene
- Freewrite 100 words (no editing)

WIP
- Doodle or brainstorm ideas
- Affirm "I am a work in progress"
- Freewrite 500 words or rework a scene

HAPPY
- Doodle your character's happy place
- Write for 60 minutes (split into 20-min sessions with breaks)
- Optional: Edit or expand on scenes

JOYFUL
- Doodle your personal happy place or story idea
- Write for 60–90 minutes (multiple sessions)
- Optional: start a second writing session
- Reflect or plan next steps

Write Draw Journal Craft Here

Writing Goals

Week: _____

Mood/Emotion Tracker

○ ○ ○ ○ ○
SAD STABLE WIP HAPPY JOYFUL
         ↔

Doodle Space:

Writing Goals for Your Project

Writing Goals for The Week:

Emotional Writing Suggestions

SAD
- Doodle or sketch something comforting
- Write down one small thing that went well today
- Work on your character's low points / conflict scenes

STABLE
- Doodle Happy Thoughts
- Read over your latest sketch or scene
- Freewrite 100 words (no editing)

WIP
- Doodle or brainstorm ideas
- Affirm "I am a work in progress"
- Freewrite 500 words or rework a scene

HAPPY
- Doodle your character's happy place
- Write for 60 minutes (split into 20-min sessions with breaks)
- Optional: Edit or expand on scenes

JOYFUL
- Doodle your personal happy place or story idea
- Write for 60–90 minutes (multiple sessions)
- Optional: start a second writing session
- Reflect or plan next steps

What I'm Proud of This Week:

Write Draw Journal Craft Here

Writing Goals

Week: _____

Mood/Emotion Tracker

○ ○ ○ ○ ○
SAD STABLE WIP HAPPY JOYFUL
         ↔

Doodle Space:

Writing Goals for Your Project

Writing Goals for The Week:

What I'm Proud of This Week:

Emotional Writing Suggestions

SAD
- Doodle or sketch something comforting
- Write down one small thing that went well today
- Work on your character's low points / conflict scenes

STABLE
- Doodle Happy Thoughts
- Read over your latest sketch or scene
- Freewrite 100 words (no editing)

WIP
- Doodle or brainstorm ideas
- Affirm "I am a work in progress"
- Freewrite 500 words or rework a scene

HAPPY
- Doodle your character's happy place
- Write for 60 minutes (split into 20-min sessions with breaks)
- Optional: Edit or expand on scenes

JOYFUL
- Doodle your personal happy place or story idea
- Write for 60–90 minutes (multiple sessions)
- Optional: start a second writing session
- Reflect or plan next steps

Write Draw Journal Craft Here

Writing Goals

Week: _____

Mood/Emotion Tracker

○ ○ ○ ○ ○
SAD STABLE WIP HAPPY JOYFUL
         ↔

Doodle Space:

Writing Goals for Your Project

Writing Goals for The Week:

What I'm Proud of This Week:

Emotional Writing Suggestions

SAD
- Doodle or sketch something comforting
- Write down one small thing that went well today
- Work on your character's low points / conflict scenes

STABLE
- Doodle Happy Thoughts
- Read over your latest sketch or scene
- Freewrite 100 words (no editing)

WIP
- Doodle or brainstorm ideas
- Affirm "I am a work in progress"
- Freewrite 500 words or rework a scene

HAPPY
- Doodle your character's happy place
- Write for 60 minutes (split into 20-min sessions with breaks)
- Optional: Edit or expand on scenes

JOYFUL
- Doodle your personal happy place or story idea
- Write for 60–90 minutes (multiple sessions)
- Optional: start a second writing session
- Reflect or plan next steps

Write Draw Journal Craft Here

Templates

Templates

The templates featured in this book are listed here. Make copies for your personal use. For best results, use a fresh journal for each new project—it helps keep your ideas, characters, and storylines organized and clear.

Write Draw Journal Craft Here

Tropes

General Story Direction

Global Story

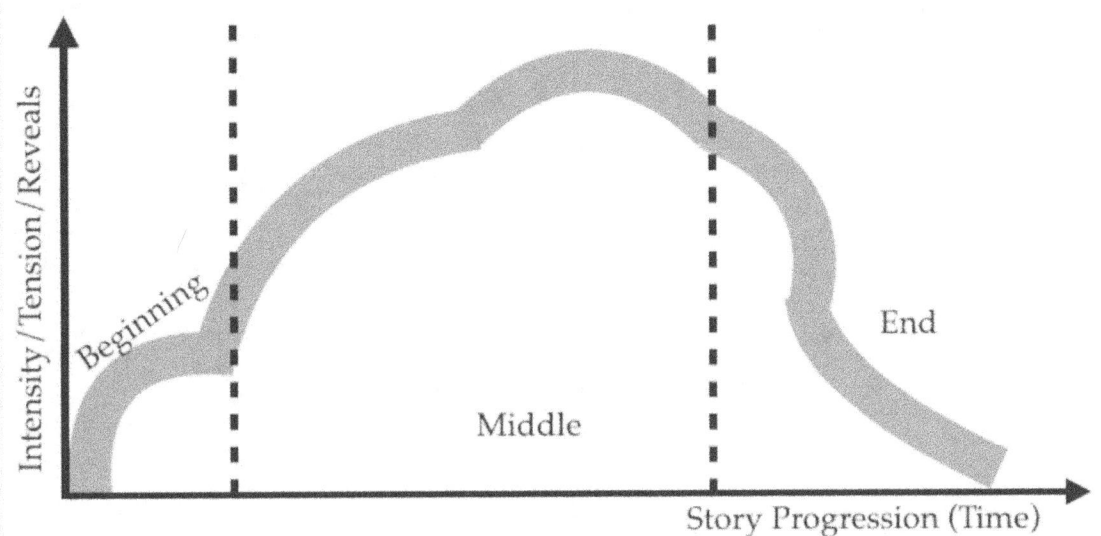

You can use more than one trope in a story, and tropes are powerful tools to drive the plot forward. Every genre has tropes—mysteries, thrillers, historical fiction, literary fiction, commercial fiction, and even nonfiction. Use them, play with them, and give them your own unique twists. Consider how a trope from one genre could add extra zing when applied to another. Romance tropes, in particular, are universal, familiar, and beloved by readers—they resonate because they tap into timeless patterns of desire, conflict, and connection. Embrace them, innovate with them, and let them enrich your storytelling.

Primary Trope:

Secondary Trope:

Additional Trope(s):

Write Draw Journal Craft Here

Names

List your favorite names for your story. Don't worry if they "fit" yet—just capture the ones that spark interest. Look up the meanings, origins, and associations (cultural, historical, symbolic). Note how these might connect to your character's personality, background, or fate. Experiment with variations (nicknames, shortened forms, translations). Sometimes the twist of a name unlocks a character. Consider sound and style—does it suit your genre? (e.g., "Lysandra" feels fantasy, while "Tommy" feels contemporary). Circle or highlight the names that feel strongest, then try them in a sentence or bit of dialogue to see if they come alive.

Name	Meaning	Nickname / Variants	Notes

Observations:

Write Draw Journal Craft Here

Attributes

Use this table to capture the key details of each of your characters. Fill in every row with what makes them visually distinct, their personality, quirks, goals, and everyday habits—anything that brings them to life on the page.

	Character Name	Character Name	Character Name
Attribute			
Eye Color			
Hair Color			
Gender			
Race/ Ethnicity			
Height			
Age			
Favorite Color			
Favorite Clothing			
Quirk			
Titles			
Profession			
Speech or Dialect			
Favorite Word(s)			
Country of Origin			

Write Draw Journal Craft Here

5 WHY'S

Journal Exercise: Digging Deeper into Motivations and Story Problems
Instructions:
1. Start with your character's surface goal (what they say they want).
2. Ask "Why?" and write the answer.
3. Ask "Why?" again—digging deeper each time.
4. Repeat at least 4-5 times until you reach an emotional or societal truth at the core.
5. This hidden truth is often where the real story tension lives.

Why is this story important?:

Why?:

Why?:

Why?:

Why?:

Observations:

Write Draw Journal Craft Here

Character Name:

Core Values

Journal Exercise: Core Values, Beliefs & Desires
Instructions:
Your character's core values and beliefs shape every decision they make—even when they don't realize it. Desires give them direction, while values and beliefs determine the choices they're willing (or unwilling) to make. Use the following questions to explore what guides your character deep down. Write freely, and don't be afraid to push for uncomfortable truths.

What principles would this character never compromise on, no matter the cost?

What does this character believe makes someone "good" or "honorable"?

What's more important to this character: truth, loyalty, or justice? Why?

Observations:

Write Draw Journal Craft Here

Character Name: **Beliefs**

Journal Exercise: Core Values, Beliefs & Desires
Instructions:
Your character's core values and beliefs shape every decision they make—even when they don't realize it. Desires give them direction, while values and beliefs determine the choices they're willing (or unwilling) to make. Use the following questions to explore what guides your character deep down. Write freely, and don't be afraid to push for uncomfortable truths.

Does your character believe in God or has religious faith? Describe this system and how it affects actions or reactions.

Does this character believe people can truly change? Why or why not?

Does this character trust the world to be fair—or unfair? How does that belief show up in their actions?

Observations:

Write Draw Journal Craft Here

Character Name:

Desires

Journal Exercise: Core Values, Beliefs & Desires
Instructions:
Your character's core values and beliefs shape every decision they make—even when they don't realize it. Desires give them direction, while values and beliefs determine the choices they're willing (or unwilling) to make. Use the following questions to explore what guides your character deep down. Write freely, and don't be afraid to push for uncomfortable truths.

What does the character want most right now?

Does this character believe people can truly change? Why or why not?

What does this character think they need to be happy—and what do they really need?

Observations:

Write Draw Journal Craft Here

Character Name:

The Web

Journal Exercise: The Web — Mapping Your Character's Connections
Instructions:
Your character doesn't exist in isolation—the people around them shape who they are, how they act, and how their story unfolds. In this exercise, you'll create a relationship web to see your character's social universe at a glance.

Step 1: Draw the Web
- Write your character's name in the center of the page.
- Around the center, add names of people connected to your character:
  - Family members (parents, siblings, extended family)
  - Friends or allies
  - Mentors, guides, or teachers
  - Rivals, enemies, or antagonists

Step 2: Reflect on Influence
Ask yourself:
- How does each person influence your character?
- Who pushes them to grow or challenges their decisions?
- Who protects them, and who frustrates or opposes them?

Step 3: Label - Use arrows, notes, or symbols to show the type of relationship (supportive, tense, complicated, loving, competitive, etc.)
- S - Stranger (Beginning)
- L - Loath
- ♥ - Love
- FE - Frienemy
- F - Friend
- M - Mom
- D - Dad
- S - Sibling
- E - Enemy
- BF - Best Friend
- R - Rival
- B - Boss
- Add to this key

Write Draw Journal Craft Here

Update Your Characters /Attributes

Use this table to capture the key details of each of your characters. Fill in every row with what makes them visually distinct, their personality, quirks, goals, and everyday habits—anything that brings them to life on the page.

	Character Name	**Character Name**	**Character Name**
Attribute			
Eye Color			
Hair Color			
Gender			
Race/ Ethnicity			
Height			
Age			
Favorite Color			
Favorite Clothing			
Quirk			
Titles			
Profession			
Speech or Dialect			
Favorite Word(s)			
Country of Origin			

Write Draw Journal Craft Here

Character Name:

The Mask – The Lie

Journal Exercise: Digging Deeper into The Lie
Instructions:
1. Every character acts through a lens—a belief that may not be true, but that shapes their choices. Remember: This isn't just backstory—this is the lens through which your character interprets every situation in your story.
2. Dig deeper:
3. Analyze the impact:

What false belief does my character cling to? Write the first answer that comes to mind.

Why do they believe this?

How does this belief protect them? (e.g., keeps them safe, avoids pain)

How does it hold them back? (e.g., prevents growth, blocks love or success)

Observations:

Write Draw Journal Craft Here

Character Name: # Goals

Journal Exercise: Defining Your Character's Goals

Instructions:

Your character's values, beliefs, and desires (from the Heartbeat section) often hint at tangible goals. Goals are what your character actively works toward—they give your story direction, tension, and stakes.

Step 1: Look Back at the Heartbeat Section
- Review the core values, beliefs, and desires you've recorded for your character.
- Identify any aspirations, wishes, or unmet needs that could become goals.

Step 2: Convert Desires into Tangible Goals
- For each potential goal, ask:
  a. Is it tangible? (Can it be clearly seen or measured?)
  b. Is it measurable? (Can you track progress or completion?)
  c. Does it have a timeline? (By when does the character aim to achieve it?)
- Only include goals that meet these criteria.

Goal	Timeline	Measurable: Name Measures or Metrics	Tangible (Y or N)	Notes

Write Draw Journal Craft Here

Character Name:

External Vs. Internal

Journal Exercise: The Storm — Obstacles & Inner Conflict

Instructions:

Step 1: Identify External Obstacles
- Who or what stands in your character's way?
- Is it a rival, a law, a lack of resources, or a dangerous environment?

Step 2: Identify Internal Conflicts
- What fears, insecurities, or false beliefs sabotage them?
- What past wounds keep resurfacing?

Obstacle / Conflict	Ext or Int	Why It Matters	How It Challenges the Character	Possible Outcome

Observations:

Write Draw Journal Craft Here

Character Name:

Strengths & Weaknesses

Journal Exercise: Digging Deeper into Motivations and Story Problems
Instructions:
List Strengths: What skills, traits, or talents make your character capable, admirable, or unique? Think both practical (good fighter, clever strategist) and personal (loyal friend, quick thinker).
List Flaws: Where do they stumble? What blind spots, habits, or weaknesses sabotage them? Which flaws are connected to their strengths?

Strengths

Weaknesses

Observations:

Write Draw Journal Craft Here

Story Arcs

Character (3):

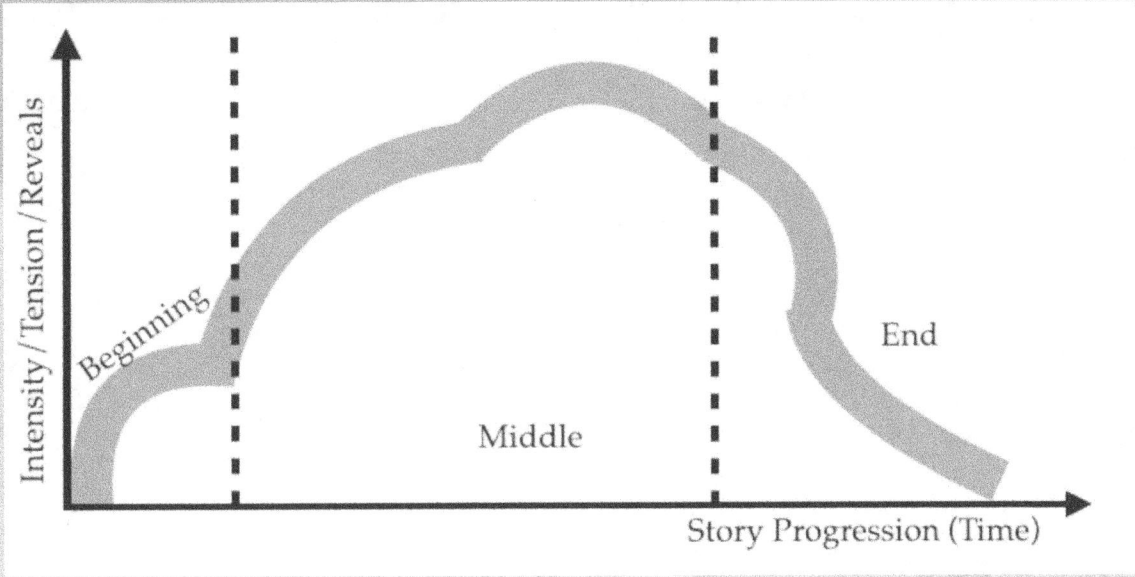

Beginning:

Middle:

End:

Write Draw Journal Craft Here

The World

Character Name:

Journal Exercise: Building the World
Instructions:
Map the world around them, filling out the table below to capture how the world influences your character? Build one for each significant location. Start global. Then do local - homes, office, etc.

City

Favorite Place

Favorite Activity

Geography - City Streets, etc.

Job

Favorite Weather

Observations:

Write Draw Journal Craft Here

Romancing the Beat

Using your answers, answer the questions for Romancing the Beat or 7 Romantic Comedy Beats

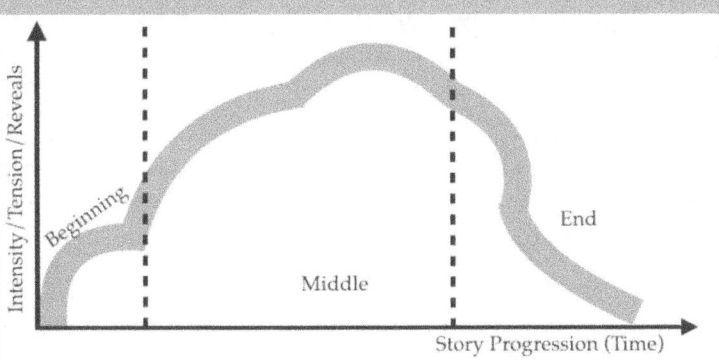

Romancing the Beat	
Introduce Hero/Heroine (Phase 1: Set Up) - Introduce the first protagonist, their ordinary life, internal struggles, external goals, and hint at what they need to grow.	
Meet Cute (Phase 1: Set Up) - The first encounter between the two protagonists, sparked by circumstance, chance, or conflict; hints at attraction and tension.	
Introduce H2 (Phase 1: Set Up) - Introduce the second protagonist in their ordinary life, showing their desires, flaws, and goals.	
No Way 1 (Phase 1: Set Up) - H1 voices their reason for avoiding love, particularly with H2, establishing initial resistance.	
Adhesion (Phase 1: Set Up) - An event forces the protagonists together, raising stakes and sparking attraction despite conflict.	
No Way 2 (Phase 2: Falling in Love) - H1 reasserts resistance; internal needs clash with external goals, keeping the romance at bay.	
Inkling of Desire (Phase 2: Falling in Love) - Characters begin admitting feelings; false beliefs are challenged.	
Deepening Desire (Phase 2: Falling in Love) - Emotional connection strengthens; protagonists reveal true selves, further eroding resistance.	

Write Draw Journal Craft Here

Romancing the Beat

Using your answers, answer the questions for Romancing the Beat or 7 Romantic Comedy Beats

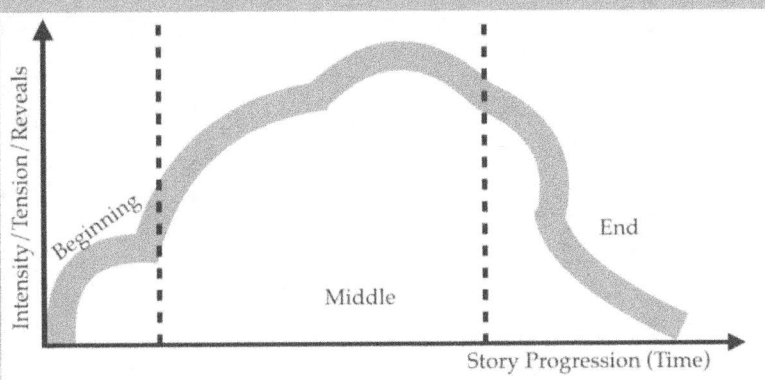

Romancing the Beat	
Maybe This Could Work (Phase 2: Falling in Love) - Protagonists question prior resistance, tension grows between feelings and goals.	
Midpoint of Love (Phase 2: Falling in Love) - A false high; protagonists glimpse the possibility of love while balancing goals and desires.	
Inkling of Doubt (Phase 3: Retreating From Love) - Old doubts and false beliefs return; characters begin pulling back.	
Deepening Doubt (Phase 3: Retreating From Love) - Intimacy continues but seeds of doubt affect the relationship.	
Retreat Beat (Phase 3: Retreating From Love) - Trust falters; characters articulate fears and protect their hearts.	
Shields Up (Phase 3: Retreating From Love) - Worst-case scenario; prior "No Way" fears seem validated, relationship breaks down.	
Break Up (Phase 3: Retreating From Love) - Relationship ends; protagonists cling to false beliefs or fears.	

Write Draw Journal Craft Here

Romancing the Beat

Using your answers, answer the questions for Romancing the Beat or 7 Romantic Comedy Beats

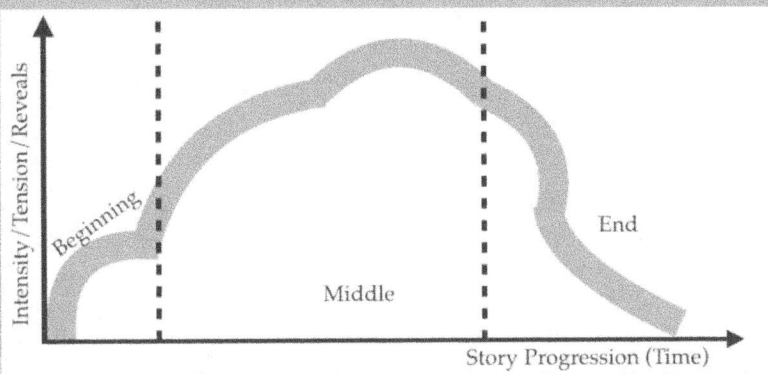

Romancing the Beat	
Dark Night (Phase 4: Fighting for Love) – "What have I done?" moment; reflection on past choices and lingering feelings.	
Wake Up (Phase 4: Fighting for Love) – Protagonist chooses love over fear; begins actively fighting for the relationship.	
Grand Gesture (Phase 4: Fighting for Love) – A dramatic act to prove commitment and overcome obstacles to love.	
What Wholehearted Looks Like (Phase 4: Fighting for Love) – Characters show personal growth and emotional transformation; relationship solidifies.	
Epilogue (Phase 4: Fighting for Love) – Return to the ordinary world, showing the protagonists' transformed selves and happy resolution.	

Write Draw Journal Craft Here

7 Romantic Comedy Beats

Using your answers, answer the questions for Romancing the Beat or 7 Romantic Comedy Beats

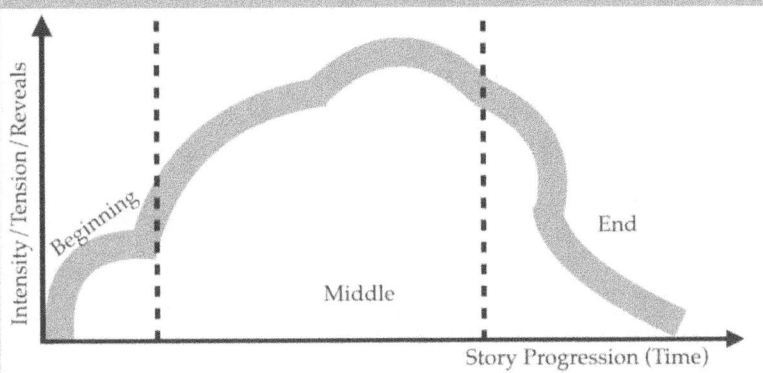

7 Romantic Comedy Beats	
The Chemical Equation (Setup) – Introduces the protagonist's internal and external conflicts and their ordinary world.	
Meet Cute (The Catalyst / Inciting Incident) – The first meeting of the protagonist and love interest, sparking conflict and/or attraction.	
A Sexy Complication (Turning Point 1) – A development that raises stakes and shows the characters at cross-purposes, building romantic tension.	
The Hook (Midpoint) – A situation binds the characters together, deepening connection while challenging beliefs or goals.	
Swivel (Turning Point 2) – The relationship's stakes peak; the romance conflicts with external goals, leading to a pivotal choice.	
Dark Moment (Crisis / Climax) – The "all is lost" moment; the relationship and/or the protagonist's goals seem doomed.	
Joyful Defeat (Resolution) – The protagonist(s) reconcile, resolve internal and external conflicts, and commit to love, often with some personal sacrifice.	

Write Draw Journal Craft Here

Romantasy Beats

Using your answers, build the Romantasy Beats.

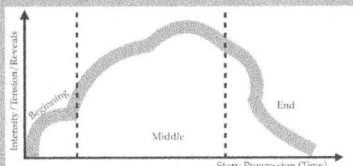

Romantasy Beats	
World & Protagonist Setup - H1 meets H2 (or is forced into proximity) through some fantasy event (e.g., curse, magical accident, alliance necessity). The catalyst disturbs both personal and world status quo.	
Meet of Love & Catalyst - H1 meets H2 (or is forced into proximity) through some fantasy event (e.g., curse, magical accident, alliance necessity). The catalyst disturbs both personal and world status quo.	
First Resistance / "No Way"- H1 resists romance due to internal beliefs/fears, responsibilities, or because romance conflicts with fantasy duty (e.g., prophecy states love must be sacrificed).	
Forced Cooperation / World Stakes Raise -External fantasy plot pushes them together—maybe to solve a magical problem, fight a common enemy, or undertake a quest. Their romantic chemistry starts under duress.	
Deepening Connection + Fantasy Conflict - They share vulnerability; fantasy stakes magnify (e.g. one's magic is dangerous or unstable). Conflict between what they want romantically vs what the world demands.	
Midpoint / False Hope A turning point where both romance & fantasy goals seem aligned—maybe a victory or breakthrough that suggests they might have both love and save the world.	
Betrayal or Dark Revelation Something is revealed about fantasy world rules, past betrayals, or magical curses that threatens trust or loyalty. The romantic relationship is tested heavily.	

Write Draw Journal Craft Here

Character Name:

The Pre – Synopsis 1

Journal Exercise: The Full Circle — Writing Your Character Synopsis
Instructions:
Now it's time to bring everything together. Using your notes from previous sections, write a short synopsis that captures your character's journey from beginning to end. This synopsis should highlight who they are, what they want, what stands in their way, and how they change.

Who is your character at the beginning (ordinary life, Spark)?

What do they believe (Heartbeat), and what lie do they carry (Mask)?

What do they want most (Flame)?

Who is in their corner or in their way (Web)?

Notes:

Write Draw Journal Craft Here

Character Name:

The Pre – Synopsis 2

Journal Exercise: The Full Circle — Writing Your Character Synopsis
Instructions:
Now it's time to bring everything together. Using your notes from previous sections, write a short synopsis that captures your character's journey from beginning to end. This synopsis should highlight who they are, what they want, what stands in their way, and how they change.

What challenges or conflicts test them (Storm)?

How do their strengths and flaws (Mirror) drive success or mistakes?

What critical moment forces them to grow (Arc)?

Notes:

Write Draw Journal Craft Here

Character Name:

The Pre – Synopsis 3

Journal Exercise: The Full Circle – Writing Your Character Synopsis
Instructions:
Now it's time to bring everything together. Using your notes from previous sections, write a short synopsis that captures your character's journey from beginning to end. This synopsis should highlight who they are, what they want, what stands in their way, and how they change.

Where does the journey leave them?

What truth replaces their lie?

How have their goals, beliefs, and relationships changed?

What final choice defines them?

Notes:

Write Draw Journal Craft Here

Mini Synopsis

Using your answers, combine everything into a 1-3 paragraph character synopsis. Write it in third person, like a back-cover blurb.

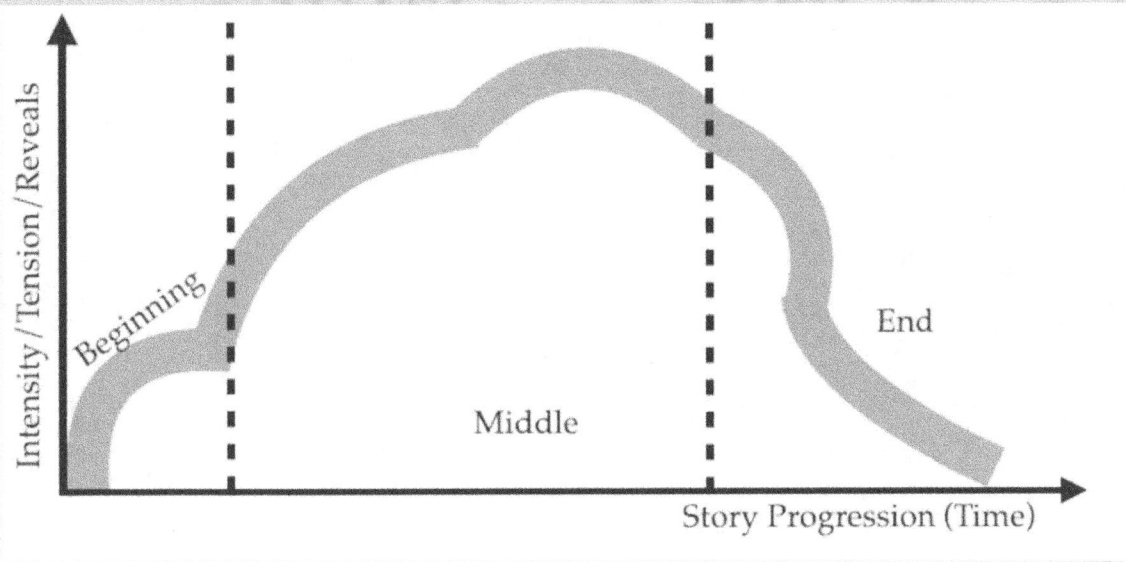

Beginning:

Write Draw Journal Craft Here

Mini Synopsis

Using your answers, combine everything into a 1-3 paragraph character synopsis. Write it in third person, like a back-cover blurb.

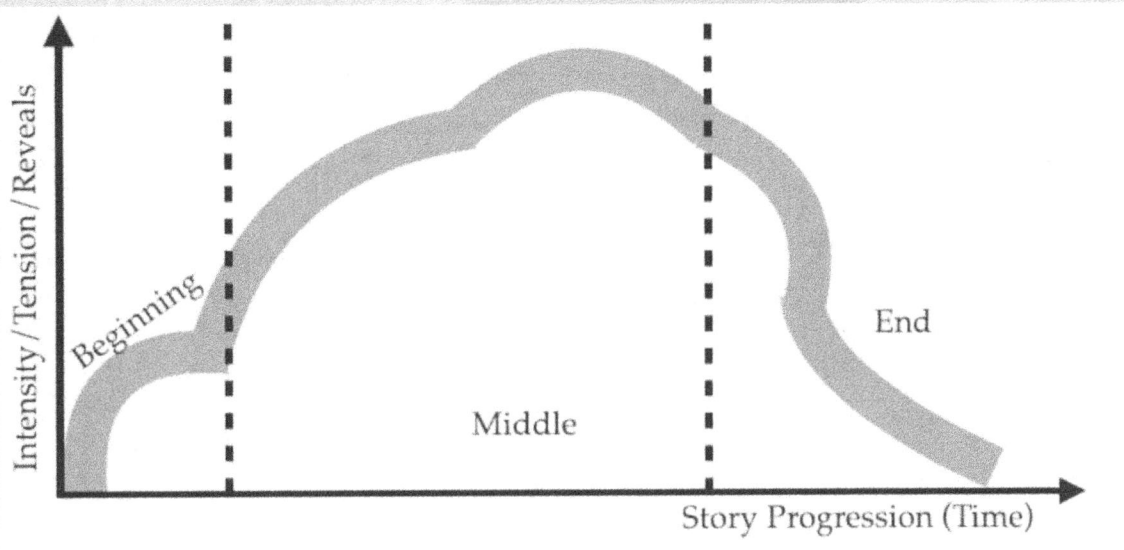

Middle:

Write Draw Journal Craft Here

Mini Synopsis

Using your answers, combine everything into a 1-3 paragraph character synopsis. Write it in third person, like a back-cover blurb.

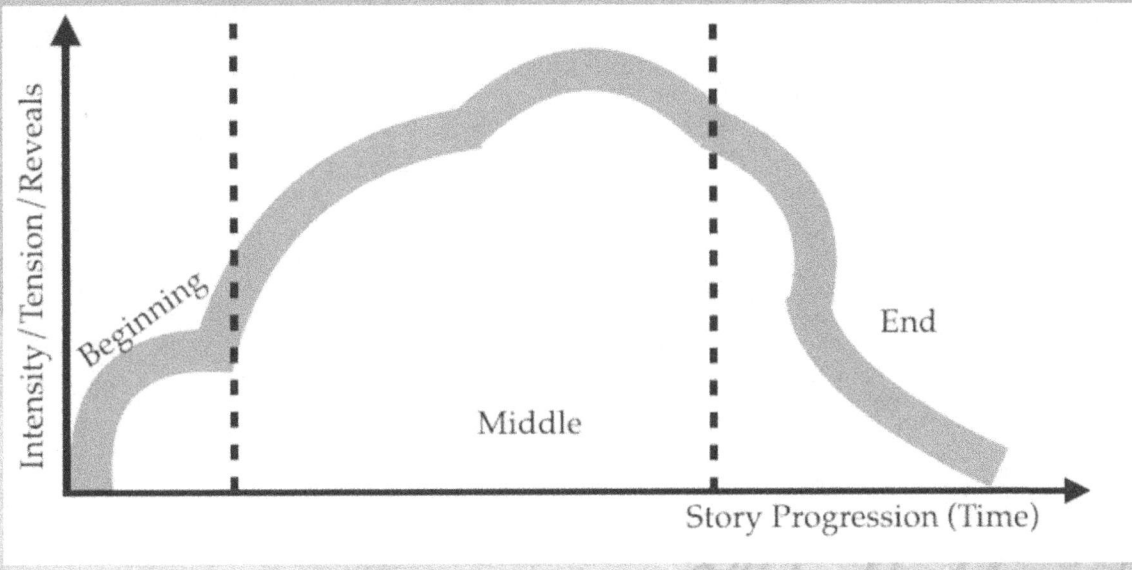

End:

Write Draw Journal Craft Here

References:

- Bowerman, Peter. The Well-Fed Writer: Financial Self-Sufficiency as a Commercial Freelancer in Six Months or Less. Fanove Publishing, 2000.
- Cowden, Victoria Lynn, and Stephanie S. Smith. 45 Master Characters: Mythic Models for Creating Original Characters. Writer's Digest Books, 2002.
- Hall, Oakley. How Fiction Works: Proven Techniques for Powerful Fiction. Writer's Digest Books, 2001.
- Kress, Nancy. Beginnings, Middles, and Ends. Writer's Digest Books, 1993.
- Leder, Meg, and Jack Heffron, editors. The Complete Handbook of Novel Writing: Everything You Need to Know to Create & Sell Your Work. Writer's Digest Books, 2002.
- Michaels, Leigh. On Writing Romance: How to Craft a Novel That Sells. Writer's Digest Books, 2007.
- Rittenberg, Ann, and Laura Whitcomb. Your First Novel: A Published Author and a Top Agent Share the Keys to Achieving Your Dream. Writer's Digest Books, 2006.
- Vogler, Christopher. The Writer's Journey: Mythic Structure for Writers. Michael Wiese Productions, 2007.

Write Draw Journal Craft Here